PROCLAMATION:
Aids for Interpreting the
Lessons of the Church Year

SERIES B

William Hordern
and
John Otwell

FORTRESS PRESS   Philadelphia, Pennsylvania

COPYRIGHT © 1975 BY FORTRESS PRESS

All rights reserved. No part of this publication may be reproduced, stored in a retrieval system, or transmitted in any form or by any means, electronic, mechanical, photocopying, recording, or otherwise, without the prior permission of the copyright owner.

Library of Congress Catalog Card Number 74-24901

ISBN 0-8006-4073-X

4697B75   Printed in U.S.A.   1-4073

General Preface

Proclamation: Aids for Interpreting the Lessons of the Church Year is a series of twenty-six books designed to help clergymen carry out their preaching ministry. It offers exegetical interpretations of the lessons for each Sunday and many of the festivals of the church year, plus homiletical ideas and insights.

The basic thrust of the series is ecumenical. In recent years the Episcopal church, the Roman Catholic church, the United Church of Christ, the Christian Church (Disciples of Christ), the United Methodist Church, the Lutheran and Presbyterian churches, and also the Consultation on Church Union have adopted lectionaries that are based on a common three-year system of lessons for the Sundays and festivals of the church year. *Proclamation* grows out of this development, and authors have been chosen from all of these traditions. Some of the contributors are parish pastors; others are teachers, both of biblical interpretation and of homiletics. Ecumenical interchange has been encouraged by putting two persons from different traditions to work on a single volume, one with the primary responsibility for exegesis and the other for homiletical interpretation.

Despite the high percentage of agreement between the traditions, both in the festivals that are celebrated and the lessons that are appointed to be read on a given day, there are still areas of divergence. Frequently the authors of individual volumes have tried to take into account the various textual traditions, but in some cases this has proved to be impossible; in such cases we have felt constrained to limit the material to the Lutheran readings.

The preacher who is looking for "canned sermons" in these books will be disappointed. These books are one step removed from the pulpit: they explain what the lessons are saying and suggest ways of relating this biblical message to the contemporary situation. As such they are springboards for creative thought as well as for faithful proclamation of the word.

The authors of this volume of *Proclamation* are William Hordern and John H. Otwell. Dr. Hordern, the editor-homiletician, is President of the Lutheran Theological Seminary, Saskatoon, Sask., Canada. He studied at the University of Saskatchewan (B.A.) and St. Andrew's College (B.D.)

and then did graduate work in theology at Union Theological Seminary, New York (Th.D.). Prior to becoming president of the Lutheran Theological Seminary in Saskatoon in 1966 he held teaching positions at Swarthmore College and Garrett Theological Seminary. He is the author of several books, the most recent being *New Directions in Theology Today* (Philadelphia: Westminster, 1966). Dr. Hordern is a member of the Evangelical Lutheran Church of Canada. Dr. Otwell, the exegete, is Professor of Old Testament at the Pacific School of Religion, Berkeley, California. He studied at Kenyon College, DePauw University (A.D.), and Garrett Biblical Institute before he moved out west to the Pacific School of Religion from which he received both the B.D. and the Th.D. degrees. Dr. Otwell has been on the faculty of the Pacific School of Religion since 1947. His most recent book is *I Will Be Your God: A Layman's Guide to Old Testament Study* (Nashville: Abingdon, 1967). Dr. Otwell is an ordained Methodist minister and an active member of The First Congregational Church of Berkeley.

Introduction

Traditionally Lent has been a period of intensive activity in our churches. In many cases it is the only period of the year during which mid-week worship services can draw a significant number of worshipers. Special giving projects often make it a crucial period for the economic well-being of the congregation. Christians have seen it as a period for self-discipline and denial, for heart-searching and repentance. But in recent years we have had a number of second thoughts about the traditional observance of Lent.

The traditional Lent was a solemn and joyless period which emphasized a sackcloth and ashes mood. Special celebrations, such as the famous Mardi Gras, were held just prior to and following the season because there was no opportunity for joy or fun during the bleak days of Lent. But in recent years we have come to appreciate the place of joy and celebration in the Christian faith. It goes against this understanding to make Lent into an orgy of gloom.

The self-sacrifices with which Lent was once observed often seem hypocritical and legalistic today. Christians solemnly decided to give up some pleasure of life for the six weeks of Lent. Often the self-denial was, in fact, good for the health or general welfare of the person and hence in no sense a real sacrifice. But in our world of hunger and starvation, it is difficult to feel righteous because, for a few weeks in the year, we cut back on the enjoyment of our affluence. The basic trouble with traditional Lenten "sacrifices" was that all too often they were aimed at enhancing the spirituality of the person making the sacrifice. But a Christian sacrifice is one that is inspired by love and is made for the sake of the persons who can be helped by the sacrifice. The self-denials of Lent all too often inspired people to look more at themselves rather than to look to their neighbors.

As Christians are wrestling with how to observe Lent today, these readings are highly significant. They do not direct our thoughts to our inner life and spiritual condition but rather they concentrate upon what God has done and is doing. In one way or another, most of these readings direct our thoughts to the covenant which God has made with his people. The word "testament" means "covenant" and it is no accident that our Bible is divided into the Old and the New Covenants. The biblical God was not content to sit in heaven and wait for human beings to turn to him. On the contrary, God took the initiative to seek all people. He entered into a covenant with Abraham and his descendants in order that through them there might be blessing for all the people of the world (Gen. 12:1-3).

A covenant implies a binding of two parties together in mutual agreement. The most widely observed covenant in human relations is the marriage covenant and so we find that again and again the Bible compares God's relationship with his people to the relationship of wives and husbands. The story of God's covenant with his people is the story of God's faithfulness to the covenant and the people's unfaithfulness. Repeatedly God renews his covenant by forgiving his people and starting anew. Most decisively this occurred in the coming of God's Son to inaugurate the new covenant that had been promised.

Because our readings for Lent are centered around the covenant, they direct our attention to God and his action. In so doing they remind us that Lent is properly observed not by intense self-examination but by lifting up our eyes to God. By concentrating upon God we are pulled out of ourselves and filled with the desire to serve God who has faithfully kept his covenant with us.

It is human nature to assume that we must repent, reform our lives, and do good works in order that God may forgive us, love us, and accept us. The net result is that whatever we do, we have one eye upon our own self-interest in the doing of it. When Lent is observed in that spirit we perform various acts of piety and self-denial in order that we may enhance our status before God. But when our attention is turned to God's covenant we find that before we have repented or performed good deeds, God has forgiven us, loved us, and accepted us. As a result we do not repent and serve God in order to win his favors but rather to express our love and gratitude to God because we have already received his favors. Lent observed in the light of the message of the covenant, therefore, pulls us out of ourselves and directs our attention to God's acts and, through them, to our neighbors whom God also loves.

Table of Contents

General Preface	iii
Introduction	v
Ash Wednesday	1
The First Sunday in Lent	9
The Second Sunday in Lent	17
The Third Sunday in Lent	25
The Fourth Sunday in Lent	34
The Fifth Sunday in Lent	42

Ash Wednesday

Lutheran	Roman Catholic	Episcopal	Pres./UCC/Chr.	Methodist/COCU
Joel 2:12-19	Joel 2:12-18	Joel 2:12-19	Isa. 58:3-12	Joel 2:12-19
2 Cor. 5:20b-6:2	2 Cor. 5:20-6:2	2 Cor. 5:20b-6:10	James 1:12-18	James 1:12-18
Matt. 6:1-6, 16-18	Matt. 6:1-6, 16-18	Matt. 6:1-6, 16-21	Mark 2:15-20	Mark 2:15-20

EXEGESIS

First Lesson: Joel 2:12-19. The word of the Lord came to Joel during a plague of locusts (1:4; 2:25) and a drought (1:17, 19 f.). These scourges have appeared often in the Near East, and references to them do not help us to date a writing. Joel 2:2 describes a rite to be performed in the temple precincts. The temple, therefore, was standing when Joel prophesied. But was it the pre-exilic structure destroyed in 586 B.C. (2 Kings 25:9) or the building erected during the Persian period? Joel 3:1 presupposes the exile following 586 B.C., yet this verse is in the part of the book containing eschatological visions held by many scholars to be of a different authorship than 1:1-2:29. In 1:1-2:29, however, Joel likened the locusts to a ravening army (2:4-9) and the drought to cosmic fire (1:19) and believed them to be manifestations of the Day of the Lord (2:10-12). The tradition of the Day of the Lord is itself eschatological, even when used by Amos (5:18-20). Thus it can be concluded that Joel 2:30 ff. is merely a spelling out of a belief already present in 1:1-2:17. This conclusion then enables us to use 3:1 to help date the prophet's ministry to the Persian period. He thus comes to us as a prophet preaching after the great age of prophecy.

The message of the book is clear. The prophet interprets the plague and drought as an hour of total judgment, the Day of the Lord. The people are called to repent (2:12-17). A second oracle announces that God has heard and will respond (2:18-27, interrupted with a summons to praise the Lord in vv. 21-23). The redemption from plague and drought are then seen to be the beginning of an outpouring of divine favor (2:28 ff.).

Joel was a cult prophet. The first word of the Lord which he proclaimed commanded a series of cultic acts: fasting, weeping, mourning, the sounding of the shophar (the ram's horn blown during the New Year's festival), the calling of a cultic assembly, and the ritual weeping of the priests before the altar. The solemnity of the summons is seen in the unusual range of those ordered to attend, everyone from nursing infants to the recently married (who normally were exempted from some public duties: Deut. 24:5). There is no indication in the surviving oracles of Joel of any understanding of the source of divine displeasure, as there so often was in the prophets of the eighth to sixth centuries B.C. Correspondingly, there is no statement of abuses to be corrected. This may reflect the limited autonomy of Jews under Persian rule. It may also be the result of the understanding of the will of the Lord that separated the cult prophet from an Amos or an Isaiah.

Nonetheless, the people are exhorted to "return to me with all your heart" and "to rend your hearts and not your garments." In biblical Hebrew, "heart" (*lebh*) refers to the physical organ, to the whole self, or to the mind or the will. The context determines the precise meaning intended. When Jeremiah proclaimed it as the will of God that the people should circumcise the foreskins of their hearts (Jer. 4:4), and Joel proclaimed that they should "rend their hearts and not their garments," a ritual act was internalized. What was done to flesh or cloth in a rite was commanded to be done to man's heart. In both instances, man's "will" would seem to be a valid translation. The rending of garments often was a part of the rite of mourning (2 Sam. 1:11; 3:31). At other times, it was either an expression of agitation as intense as mourning (2 Sam. 13:19) or a form of self-abasement (1 Kings 21:27; 2 Kings 5:7 f.). Here, the phrase "rend your hearts" is an exhortation to subdue the will.

Fasting, weeping, mourning, and the rending of the heart are elaborations of the twice-repeated command "to return." In the first appearance of the exhortation, the people are urged to return "with all your heart," i.e., decisively and without qualifications. In the second, they are asked to return to "the Lord your God." The deity to whom they are to turn is thus identified precisely and in a title with strong convenantal associations.

Each renewal of the exhortation to return (vv. 12, 13ab, 15-17) is balanced by a divine response. Joel first encouraged the hope that God might respond to the people's turning to him by turning toward them (*shubh*, "to turn," commanded of the people in 12b and 13c is applied to God in 14a). In vv. 18 f., the hope voiced in vv. 13 f. becomes the proclamation that the Lord will act. The restoration promised is the revival of the productivity of the land.

Second Lesson: 2 Cor. 5:20b—6:2. During the course of his turbulent relations with the church at Corinth, Paul found his authority as an apostle and the standing of his fellow workers challenged by persons from Jerusalem who claimed a higher authority for themselves (cf. 2 Cor. 11:5, 13; 12:11; 13:2 f.). These verses are part of his defense of his mission. In 5:20a, Paul applies the term *presbeuomen* to himself and his co-workers, rather than *apostolos*. *Presbeuomen* was the title borne by representatives of the Roman Senate charged with making peace with a defeated enemy or by the representative of the emperor in an imperial province. Since Paul and his co-workers were pleading for reconciliation between God and man, the peace-making role of the senatorial representatives may have been uppermost in his mind.

The means by which the relationship between God and man is to be restored is described tersely in v. 21. God adjudged Christ to be sinful so that we, who are sinful, could achieve mystical union with Christ ("be in Christ"). But there is no estrangement between God and Christ since Christ "knew no sin." As we come to be "in Christ," we become "a new creation" (v. 17) because we share Christ's true nature and are accepted into the unbroken relationship between God and Christ.

As a co-worker with Christ, Paul pleads in 6:1 that the Corinthians should avoid accepting the salvation which God has offered in such a way as to invalidate it. Rather, they should receive it now, on the day that it is offered them (quoting Isa. 49:2).

Gospel: Matthew 6:1-6, 16-18. These sayings are found only in the Gospel of Matthew and thus may have come either from oral tradition or from a written source used only by this evangelist. They are a part of the Sermon on the Mount, a collection of teachings reported in this Gospel to have been given by Jesus to his disciples after he and they had withdrawn from the crowds to a mountain top. Since parallels to many of the sayings in the Sermon on the Mount appear in different contexts in Luke, it is likely that the Sermon on the Mount is a collection of utterances by Jesus removed from their original settings. The intention of the Matthean collection may have been to portray Jesus as a new Moses founding a new Israel and giving it laws.

Three rites are discussed: almsgiving (6:2-4), prayer (6:5-6), and fasting (6:16-18). All were well established in Judaism, and the validity of each is assumed here. All, however, are described as invalid when performed for human approval (6:1).

Vv. 2, 5, and 16 contain a formula: the disciples are urged not to be like the *hypokritēs* who "have received their reward." Our word hypocrite is a transliteration of the Greek *hypokritēs*, but *hypokritēs* could mean interpreter, orator, or actor, as well as one claiming moral or spiritual excellence falsely. The phrase "they have received their reward" seems virtually to have been a technical term for a legally valid receipt.

The significance of the sounding of the trumpet before giving alms is unclear. It may have been intended merely to indicate ostentation, but such exaggeration would be out of character with the naturalism of the parables. It has been suggested that it is a reference to the blowing of trumpets during a Jewish ritual. We know nothing of a ritual for almsgiving, however. Trumpet blasts were sounded in the temple during the payment of the temple tax, and the limits put upon the number of blasts permitted suggests that ostentation had become a problem (Mishnah: Arakhin 3, 5). The payment of the temple tax was not almsgiving, however. Apuleius, writing shortly after A.D. 150, described the sounding of a trumpet between dances and the play which followed (*The Golden Ass*, Bk X).

V. 16 is not wholly clear. It is widely held that the disfiguring of the faces of the *hypokritēs* during fasting was done either by facial expression or the use of ashes. The Greek verb means to cover, or to conceal, and again there seems to be an exaggeration: to use so much dirt that the face was hidden. It should be noted that actors in classical antiquity wore masks on stage.

There seems to have been no Jewish drama until well into the Christian Era. The theater was so prominent in Graeco-Roman culture, however, that many of its features would probably have been known to Jews who would have rejected it both because of its immorality and its Hellenistic associations. The remains of Roman theaters can still be seen in such sites as Gadara and Scythopolis in Galilee. All three of the sayings before us contain material consistent with the hypothesis that their intended context was the Hellenistic stage: the trumpet blasts before the actor begins, the translation of *hypokritēs* as actor, the emphasis on a human audience, and the concealment of the face of the *hypokritēs*. Two of these features create difficulties (one insoluble) if the context is held to be first century Palestinian Jewish life.

If these three sayings are interpreted as suggested here, the condemnation of acts of piety performed to gain status in man's eyes gains intensity. The almsgiving, prayer, and fasting not only are directed toward the wrong recipient, the only comparison appropriate to describe them is the degenerate theater of the Roman empire. The applause of the human spectators is the full and sole payment.

In contrast to practices which have a high visibility for men, Jesus commended forms of these rites which concealed their practice from others, the better to insure their performance solely for God. His teaching that alms should be given so surreptitiously that one hand did not know what the other had done is even more inward than the Jewish practice mentioned in Mishnah, Shekalim 5, 6, of leaving alms in a special chamber in the temple where the worthy needy could go privately to help themselves. The commandment on prayer has the effect of making it a private rite. The preparation for fasting (v. 17) would effectively conceal its presence since anointing one's head and washing one's face would be proper preparation for a wedding rather than for fasting.

In each case, the motivation for the radical change in the form of the rite is the same: the relationship between man and God is intensely private even though the consequences of it are not so restricted.

HOMILETICAL INTERPRETATION

As we noted in the Introduction, Lent is the time in the Church Year that has been particularly associated with repentance and renewal of spiritual life. It is a time when Christians have examined their lives, confessed their sins, performed acts of penitence, undertaken rigorous acts of piety such as fasting, and given more generously. It is fitting, therefore, that the scriptural passages assigned for the first day in Lent should direct our thoughts to these themes. Our readings remind us that the performance of such actions is not necessarily a sign of spiritual health. In fact, such apparently good deeds may separate us from God. These readings for Ash Wednesday force us to look past the mere performance of certain actions and ask about their motivation.

Repentance is taken for granted as a good and necessary thing in religious circles. A person who repents loudly often gains far more prestige in religious communities than the person who has no lurid past to narrate. Christians often play games with each other in which they try to establish that "I am more repentant than thou." In a similar way other acts of piety, such as giving alms, praying or fasting, can be used to gain public approval and prestige. Politicians who carefully end their political speeches with reference to the Deity are by no means alone in using piety for personal advantage.

Both the OT Lesson and the Gospel for Ash Wednesday speak out ·against the use of repentance or piety for ulterior motives. Joel calls upon the people to "rend your hearts and not your garments." True repentance, the prophet is saying, is not a matter of dramatic public acts but a matter of the whole will and self of the person. (See exegesis.) In the same vein,

Jesus calls his followers to be so secretive in their piety that not even their left hands will know what the right hands are doing.

Jesus says that those who engage in dramatic acts aimed to win public approval "have their reward." That is, they get what they are seeking—they win the approval of the uncritical public. They establish their names as people of great piety. Over against this, Jesus calls us to come to God in secret. Such piety or repentance will win no public approval or prestige. But Jesus says that God, who sees the secret action, will reward us. God's reward is not of the kind that the hypocrites receive; it does not raise us higher on the social ladder or shower us with material wealth and reward. God's reward consists of the relationship with himself. To the people who live for the things of the world, this will not seem like a reward at all. But the person of faith will ask, what higher reward could there be than the wondrous glory of being in fellowship with God?

In Lent, as we search our lives, we find that all too much of our piety is not directed towards God himself but has an eye upon a host of extraneous rewards. When we repent it is not that we are really sorry that we have sinned, it is just that we fear that we shall have to pay the consequences of our sin. Like a boy who has been caught stealing candy, we are very sorry, sorry that we have been caught, but not sorry that we have committed the sin. Similarly, whether we are praying, fasting, or giving to the poor, we have one eye upon a host of ways in which we hope to reap benefits for ourselves. When the chips are down, in religion as in the rest of our life, we ask, "What is in it for me?" What can we do to move ourselves out of this self-seeking piety so that we find our "reward" solely in the joy of the relationship between God and ourselves? It is easy to rend our garments and make a great show of repentance, but how do we manage to rend our hearts? How do we find sufficient reward in knowing that we are related to God in the secrecy of our room? The answer is obvious: there is nothing that we can do to change the basic orientation of our lives. We are self-centered individuals and so even in our religion we are seeking to promote our own advantage.

This is why the Protestant Reformers emphasized that we cannot save ourselves by our works. By an effort of our wills we can bring ourselves to do a number of things. We can rend our garments, we can give to the hungry, and we can pray and fast. But the Reformers recognized that true righteousness does not consist of going through motions, even if the motions consist of such good things as these. Luther reminds his readers again and again that true righteousness is never a matter of doing certain good deeds, but of deeds that are performed with a willing, joyful, and

Ash Wednesday

glad heart. We cannot save ourselves by our works, for although we can make ourselves do a number of fine works, we cannot make ourselves do them for the right reasons.

Joel does not leave the appeal to "rend your hearts and not your garments" stand alone as a commandment over the people. Immediately Joel goes on to add, "Return to the Lord, your God, for he is gracious and merciful, slow to anger, and abounding in steadfast love, and repents of evil" (v. 13). These words remind Joel's hearers that God is "your God." That is, he is the Lord who has called his people into the covenant relationship with himself. He is the God who has shown himself to be loving and forgiving. No matter how the people might try to repent honestly and completely, they could not succeed in doing so by their own efforts. But when they are reminded of God's steadfast love, when they experience his amazing willingness to forgive his stiff-necked and stubborn people, their hearts are moved. They are moved by God's love to respond with love, their hearts are won so that they are pulled outside of themselves. And then they become truly sorry for what they have done and for what they are. And thus God's love moves them to rend their hearts rather than their garments.

Paul's passage in 2 Cor. 5:20b—6:2 places Joel's point in light of the New Covenant that comes in Jesus Christ. Paul calls his readers to be reconciled to God because of what God already has done to reconcile them. "For our sake he made him to be sin who knew no sin, so that in him we might become the righteousness of God" (v. 21). We cannot change our inner lack of motivation by an effort of will. But what we cannot do for ourselves has been done for us in God's sacrificial approach to his people through Jesus Christ.

These readings for Ash Wednesday speak to us about how we may properly keep Lent. Traditionally we have been led to think that in Lent we should spend a great deal of time in taking a critical look at ourselves. This is not necessarily a bad thing to do, but it is dangerous. It can very easily lead us into an outward form of repentance or of piety. It leads to a rending of garments rather than hearts. True repentance and true piety are much more likely to come if we do not begin with looking at ourselves. In Lent we ought to begin by recalling the steadfast love whereby God originally called his people and the forgiveness that he extended continually to them when they fell away from him. We ought to recall how God has acted to reconcile us through Jesus Christ. When the meaning of God's love begins to come home to us, and only then, we shall begin to rend our heart, not our garments. We shall serve God in secret because the only reward that we seek is the parent-child relationship into which he has called us.

There was a time in the ministry of Jesus when his disciples began to see the impossibility of saving themselves and they asked him, "Who then can be saved?" Jesus responded, "With men this is impossible, but with God all things are possible." (Matt. 19:25-26.) Our readings for Ash Wednesday drive home this point to us. If in Lent we spend our time simply in looking at ourselves we can do no more than rend our garments. Only if we concentrate upon God and what he has done and is doing for us will we be pulled out of our self-centeredness and into the relationship with him in which we shall truly repent and truly serve him.

The First Sunday in Lent

Lutheran	Roman Catholic	Episcopal	Pres./UCC/Chr.	Methodist/COCU
Gen. 22:1-14	Gen. 9:8-15	Gen. 22:1-14	Gen. 9:8-15	Gen. 9:8-15
Rom. 8:31-39	1 Pet. 3:18-22	Rom. 4:2-3, 20-25	1 Pet. 3:18-22	1 Pet. 3:18-22
Mark 1:12-15	Mark 1:12-15	Mark 1:9-13	Mark 1:12-15	Mark 1:12-15

EXEGESIS

First Lesson: Gen. 22:1-14. This story, often described as the noblest of the patriarchal narratives, is from the Elohist (E) Pentateuchal source. The use of Yahweh in vv. 11, 14 is the work of the editor who merged this material into the Yahwist (J) source.

Gen. 22:1-14 is a saga, a narrative in which all of the skills of the storyteller were used to make a point. There are only five actors, two of whom (God and Abraham) wholly dominate. Dramatic tension is built up through the brief conversations, the pacing of the events, the lack of realism in crucial details, the vocabulary, and the incongruity of the role of God. Thus each of the terms used by God to describe Abraham's son magnifies the enormity of the command that Isaac be sacrificed, and the terse description of events early in the story contrasts with the fuller reporting as Abraham prepared to sacrifice Isaac. The impossibility of the child carrying enough wood to burn his body (v. 6) would have been obvious to the audience, and it must have been a calculated exaggeration. And were sacrificial animals killed after being bound and placed on the altar (v. 9; cf. Lev. 1:3-9)? All of these traits indicate that we have before us a skillfully told story.

Many of the details are significant. "God" in v. 1 is given the definite article and is at the beginning of the clause where the verb normally stands. Thus "God" is given such emphasis that we are warned that the primary concern throughout will be with him. His intent is "to test" Abraham's faith (the "tempt" of AV is a now archaic usage meaning "to test"). The description of the child (v. 2), "your son, your only son Isaac, whom you love," both conveys the magnitude of the test and implies the anguish of the father. The location of "the land of Moriah" is unknown. It cannot be Jerusalem (cf. 2 Chron. 3:1) because it is a land, not a mountain. The locality may have been fictitious, a further indication that this is a saga, not history.

We are struck by the pathos of the conversation in vv. 7 f. between the father, who knows the purpose of the journey, and the son, who was to be the victim. Abraham's reply to Isaac contains the first appearance of *r'h*, translated in the RSV in v. 8 as "provide," in v. 12 as "fear," and in v. 13 as "looked." *r'h* then appears twice in v. 14, once in the place name and once in the concluding proverb where it is in the passive mode (both are translated in the RSV as "provide"). Since the basic meaning of the Hebrew root *r'h* is "to see," the original force of the saga would be better preserved with translations which have been proposed by commentators for decades: in v. 8, "God will see for himself the lamb," in v. 12, "I know that you see God," in v. 13, "looked," in v. 14a, "the name of that place, 'The Lord sees,' " and in v. 14b (with emended text), "on this mount the Lord is seen."

Gen. 12:1-14 seems to preserve a tradition with the following history. In its earlier form, it was a tradition about a shrine where God sees and is seen, perhaps through human sacrifice. The Elohist transformed the shrine tradition. He first intensified the magnitude of the divine command. Abraham is asked not only for the sacrifice of a son, but of the son through whom the divine promise of progeny would have had to have come. Abraham's obedience, carried to the point where he had raised his arm to strike, became the occasion for a theophany. The supreme sacrifice of man, to which God responds by appearing, is changed from human sacrifice to the sacrifice of total obedience.

Second Lesson: Rom. 8:31-39. In these verses, Paul concludes his argument for justification through faith in Christ rather than by the doing of the law. He does not recapitulate his earlier argument. Instead, he states what is to him the significance of what has been presented, and he does it with such intensity of conviction that his words take on a hymnic tone.

The question in v. 31b, "If God be for us, who can be against us," seems at first to be incomprehensible. The persecutions Paul and his fellow Christians had already experienced surely were adequate proof to them that there were those who were against them!

The interrogative pronoun "who" (*tis*) reappears at the beginning of vv. 33, 34, 35. It designates someone, or something over against the God "who is for us" and remains unidentified until the end of the passage (vv. 35-39). There, Paul provides an inclusive catalogue of seven kinds of suffering (v. 35b, expanded by a quotation from Ps. 44:22 in v. 36), seven superhuman entities (vv. 38 f.), as well as "death or life" and "anything else in all creation." It is this baneful host which "is against us" (v. 31b), seeks to "bring ... (a) charge against" us (v. 33), "condemns us" (v. 34), and attempts to "separate us from the love of Christ" (v. 35). Thus Paul groups together both adversities and adversaries. These are the antagonists who seek to alienate Christians from God and from the love of Christ.

The proclamation of divine love, implied in the first clause of v. 31b, is described in three different ways before the final affirmation of it at the end of the passage.

The first is the evocation of Gen. 22:1-14 in v. 31. This is a study in contrasts. Abraham acted in response to divine command; God acted on his own initiative. Abraham did not complete his act; God sacrificed his son. Abraham demonstrated his faithfulness to God; God demonstrated his love for mankind. The second is the image of the trial in vv. 33, 34a in which God is the judge who has already decided against those who accuse. It should be remembered that the judge in antiquity presided over a trial; he (or they, in ancient Israel) evaluated testimony, pronounced, and executed sentence. The third is the description of Christ as the advocate (v. 34). Paul's knowledge of the Scriptures would make him familiar with the dual role of God in trial scenes in which he was both the accused and the judge (e.g., Jer. 2:5-13), or accuser and judge (e.g., Isa. 41:21-29). Here, however, God is judge only. Christ, risen from the dead and seated in a place of honor in the heavenly court, is the Christian's advocate. A check with the various versions will demonstrate that the Greek text here can be translated either as a declaration or a question. The choice ultimately is exegetical, and the exposition given here calls for a declaratory rendering (with AV, RSV margin, NEB).

Gospel: Mark 1:12-15. Mark 1:12-15 contains two of the three stages of the Markan prologue to the ministry of our Lord: the baptism (1:1-11), the temptation (1:12 f.), and the introduction to Jesus' Galilean ministry (1:14 f.). The second stage is set off from the first by a change in word order and tense. In the verses with which we are concerned, the Markan temptation story is so much shorter than the accounts in Matt. 4:1-11 and Luke 4:1-13 that it may be simpler to posit a separate tradition rather than a Markan editing of a single temptation tradition. The beginning of the Galilean ministry is reported in all four Gospels, with Mark and Matthew giving a summary of the content of Jesus' message. This is given in fuller form in Mark than in Matthew.

A sense of urgency infuses the Gospel of Mark, and it appears first in the story of the temptation. The spirit came upon Jesus with such force that he was driven at once into the wilderness. The verb used here is employed elsewhere in the Gospel for the expulsion of demons and conveys a sense of irresistible power. The dynamism of the spirit recalls its role in such OT passages as 1 Kings 18:12 and Ezek. 3:14 f.

In the scriptural tradition to which the author of Mark was heir, the attitude toward the wilderness was ambivalent. It could be remembered as the place in which Israel had had (or would again have) a special relationship to God (Exodus 19; Hos. 2:14; Jer. 2:2 f., etc.). It was a place where Israel repeatedly had rebelled against God (Ezek. 20:13-22; Psalm 78). It also was a hostile place to be feared (Jer. 2:6) in which wild animals and demonic powers lived (Isa. 34:8-14).

A forty day interval is reported in Moses' stay on Sinai (Exod. 34:28) and Elijah's flight from Jezebel (1 Kings 19:8). It should be noted that Moses and Elijah emerged from their solitude with their missions clarified and matured.

The verb "to tempt" (*peirazo*) in v. 13 is used in the Septuagint to translate the *nissah* ("to tempt") in Gen. 22:1. Satan appears in Job 1:6-8 and Zech. 3:1 f. as an angel of testing or of accusing man on God's behalf. Only later (in such intertestamental writings as The Assumption of Moses 10:1, Lives of Adam and Eve 9:1, and 2 Enoch 29:4 f., where it is Satanail) is Satan the antagonist to God he has become in the Gospels. Since wild animals were sometimes described as a part of the kingdom of evil (Ps. 22:13, 21) over which the righteous will triumph (Ps. 91:13), it is likely that the presence of wild beasts with Jesus in the wilderness is a further description of the kingdom of evil by which he was beset. The angels serve him throughout his trial (not merely at its end, as in Matt. 4:11).

Mark 1:14 f. is the introduction to Jesus' Galilean ministry. There is no report of John the Baptist's ministry (as in Matt. 3:7-12 and Luke 3:7-18), merely the notation that Jesus' ministry began after John's had ended. Although it is possible to interpret v. 14 as suggesting that Jesus had been with John earlier (as intimated in John 1:29-42), the context more naturally suggests that Jesus came to Galilee immediately after the temptation in the wilderness.

V. 15 represents a summary of the early church's understanding of the essence of Jesus' proclamation. The phrase "gospel of God" appears in 1 Thess. 2:2, 8 f.; 2 Cor. 11:7; Rom. 1:1; 15:16, and the summons to repent occurs both in Petrine and Pauline speeches in Acts (5:31; 11:18; 20:21). "Kingdom" (*basileia*) is better understood as rule or reign (so Moffat and Goodspeed). The word translated as "time" (*kairos*) is used in the Septuagint for the Hebrew *eth*. An *eth* is a unit of time bearing a distinctive character (as in Eccl. 3:2-9 where a sequence of such "times" is given).

The First Sunday in Lent

Thus the proclamation asserts that the time in which God's will will be done is close at hand. Confronted by the immanence of the breaking-in of divine sovereignty, man is summoned to repent.

HOMILETICAL INTERPRETATION

It is natural that human beings search to find a religion of "glory." That is, they seek a religion that will obviously shower them with blessings of health, wealth, and happiness. They do not want a "peace that passes understanding" (Phil. 4:7), they want a peace which everyone can understand as peace. Naturally when we try to win converts to our faith, it is most tempting to hold out promises that acceptance of our faith will bring the converts success beyond their dreams. We appeal to the natural urges of the prospective convert by trying to show that it pays to be religious.

In the season of Lent we are reminded that Christianity is not a religion of glory, it is a religion of the cross. All three of the Scripture selections for this Sunday help us to understand what this means. In three different ways they raise the problem that Christians must always face: again and again our experience in life seems to contradict our faith. In the face of so much suffering, evil, and adversity, how can we believe in God's goodness? How dare we affirm that he is a God of love?

Abraham had been called from out of his native land and given the promise that through his descendants God would bring a blessing to all the peoples of the earth (Gen. 12:1-3). Abraham was to be the father of the people chosen by God to be his covenant people. But Abraham had no children and as the years passed and his wife, Sarah, moved past the child-bearing age, it began to appear that the promise would not be kept. Just as it seemed that God had forgotten his promise, a son was born to Abraham and Sarah miraculously in their old age. Isaac, the son, was thus the link between Abraham and the promised people, he was the living sign that God would keep his promise.

It is against this background that we must see the twenty-second chapter of Genesis. God tests Abraham by asking him to sacrifice his son. To any parent this would be a painful test of faith. Down through the centuries parents have been asked to sacrifice their sons for the sake of their countries. When the grim word has come, "killed in action," most parents have wondered deep in their hearts how God could allow such things to happen. They have asked how they could continue to believe that God is good and loving. But in Abraham's case the problem went even deeper. Not only was he, a parent, asked to sacrifice his son, but this was the son of the promise. If Isaac were dead there would no longer be any reason to believe that God would keep his promise to make a covenant with Abraham and his descendants. How can Abraham keep his faith in such a situation? How can he trust a God who cannot seem to make up his mind?

Paul, in the conclusion to Romans 8 faces all of those things in life that seem to deny God and his goodness. Paul does not promise his readers that Christians will be spared from any of the tragedies that fall upon other people. He assumes that Christians, like others, will know tribulations, distress, persecution, famine, nakedness, peril, and death. If all of these adversities fall alike upon the just and the unjust, the good and the evil, then to the wisdom of the world it would not appear that it pays to be good.

Mark, in his succinct way, sums up the beginning of Jesus' ministry. When Jesus was baptized by John he received, like Abraham before him, God's word of promise. And like Abraham, he was tested. Immediately he was driven by the Spirit into the wilderness to be tempted by Satan. At the baptism Jesus had been told that he was God's beloved Son in whom God was pleased (Mark 1:11), and yet here he was being tempted like any other human being. Surely there must have been times during the forty days in the wilderness when Jesus asked whether, in light of what was happening to him, he could take seriously God's words about his sonship. And the problem did not end when Jesus came out of the wilderness because he was met with the news that John had been cast into prison. Could Jesus hear of this without knowing in his heart that it was a foreshadowing of what fate would hold in store for him too?

All three of these passages squarely face the fact that Christianity is not a religion of glory. In our sinful hearts we all desire a God who will be on our side, a God who will use his omnipotent power to protect us from the ills that beset those around us. Jesus, however, again and again warned those who would follow him that they had to take up their crosses, and these three Scripture passages help us to see the meaning of the cross that lies at the center of Christian discipleship. Christian faith is not a form of magic that will preserve the true believers from the slings and arrows of an outrageous fortune. On the contrary, it would seem that the believers may be in for more than their share of the trials and tribulations of life.

But our three selections for this Sunday have more to say than that our faith will not protect us from the woes of life. Each of them also affirms that it is precisely in the moments of trial and testing that the triumph of faith appears. Abraham goes out to sacrifice his son, hoping against hope.

The First Sunday in Lent

And at the last dramatic moment, God provides the ram as the alternative sacrifice. Paul lists the problems that the Christian will face in order to affirm that none of these is able to separate us from God's love. The love of God that is manifested in Jesus Christ is a love that carries us victoriously through all of life's tribulations. Jesus emerges from his temptations and, despite John's arrest, he proclaims that "The time is fulfilled, and the kingdom of God is at hand, repent and believe in the good news." It was precisely in and through the temptations that Jesus saw most clearly the reality of God and his kingdom.

The Christian can continue to believe in God's love despite all that seems to deny it because the Christian knows that God himself has suffered and continues to suffer with us. As the exegesis points out, in Rom. 8:31-32 Paul is obviously evoking the story of Abraham and Isaac as a background for his affirmation that nothing can separate us from God's love. The Christian cannot read about Abraham's testing without remembering that God gave his own Son and there was no ram offered as a substitute. During World War Two a story was told about a Sunday School class that was studying the crucifixion of Jesus. When finally the teacher had finished telling how Jesus died one little boy leaped up in anger and cried out, "But where were the marines?" And that is the point of Christian faith. Jesus died without the marines coming in for the last minute rescue. No legion of angels intervened to rescue God's Son from the cross. Had an intervention saved Jesus, Christianity would have been a religion of glory rather than a religion of the cross. We would seek the evidence of God in our triumphs and successes. But because God did not spare his own Son we dare to find God's love in our sufferings and defeats.

The religion of glory always wants to have Easter without Good Friday. The Greek philosophers denied that God could suffer. To them it seemed obvious that an omnipotent God could not share the finite and human weakness of suffering. But Christianity is a religion of the cross because it is the Good News of a God who did not stay in the remote protection of heaven, far from the struggle of earth. On the contrary, God came into our life through his Son and here he drank to the full the cup of suffering, temptation and sorrow. Jesus could call his followers to take up their crosses because first he bore his own cross. Similarly, God's love can come to us in our sufferings precisely because God himself has first suffered in, with, and for us.

Suffering, particularly the suffering of the relatively innocent, remains the greatest barrier to believing in God. Down through the centuries human wisdom has argued that if God is all good and all powerful, there would be no suffering. Since there is suffering either God is not all powerful or he is not all good. Most modern forms of atheism put a great deal of emphasis upon the facts of suffering in the world.

Paul found the answer to suffering in God's love from which none of the adversities of life and death can separate us. It is important, however, to see what kind of an answer this is. It is not a philosophical answer which enables us to understand the whys and wherefores of suffering. Rather it is an answer that comes from out of the experience of life itself. A few years ago I visited a woman who was dying a painful death from cancer. I marvelled to see that in the midst of her suffering she had a radiant and triumphant faith in God's love. The next day I sat in a religion seminar on a college campus where the students were arguing that it was impossible to believe in God because of the suffering in the world. I could not help but compare the two events. The dying woman, in the very midst of her suffering, knew the love of God and gratefully expressed her thanks to God for his goodness. The students, most of whom had no firsthand knowledge of any real suffering, could not believe in God because of the suffering in the world. What was the difference? The students were wrestling with a philosophical question upon the intellectual level alone. On that level, we have few answers. But the woman was speaking from out of her experience of life, suffering and approaching death. In her experience she had found the answer that philosophy still seeks. She knew in her life the love of God in Christ and because she knew it, she had an answer to suffering. It was not an answer to a philosophical question, it was an answer to a problem of life. It did not give her any glib solutions to intellectual puzzles but it enabled her to live and die victoriously. That is the nature of a religion of the cross.

The Second Sunday in Lent

Lutheran	Roman Catholic	Episcopal	Pres./UCC/Chr.	Methodist/COCU
Gen. 28:10-17	Gen. 22:1-2, 9a, 10-13, 15-18	Gen.28:11-17	Gen. 22:1-2, 9-13	Gen. 28:10-17
Rom. 5:1-11	Rom. 8:31b-34	Rom. 10:8-13	Rom. 8:31-39	Rom. 8:31-39
Mark 8:31-38	Mark 9:1-9	John 2:13-22	Mark 9:1-9	Mark 10:32-45

EXEGESIS

First Lesson: Gen. 28:10-17. Gen. 28:10-17 is a passage in which J and E, the two major narrative strands of the Pentateuch, have been fused. The identification of the once separate sources is based upon the changes in the name of deity, the twice-reported response of Jacob to his encounter with God (vv. 16 and 17), and the different content of each strand.

Vv. 10-12, 17 are assigned to E. Fleeing from Esau, Jacob, while en route from Beer-sheba to Haran, stopped for the night at an unnamed but specific place. It is mentioned twice in v. 11 ("a certain place," "the place" RSV), as is also the time of day ("that night," "to sleep"). A stone made an odd pillow, and Jacob's sleep was enlivened by the dream of a ramp or stairway extending from earth to heaven on which angels ascended and descended. The Hebrew term is derived from the root *sll* which means "to heap up," "to raise." The angels—not winged beings in the OT—used the ramp to come and go from heaven to earth. The word translated here as angel designates a messenger or agent. Jacob's response, according to E (v. 17), was fear. He recognized the place to be "the house of God" (*Beth-el*), "the gateway to heaven."

Some are tempted to see in this story only a survival of an ancient belief that one could receive a vision of a god dwelling in a stone while sleeping in the shrine at Bethel, but we must grant our narrator more subtlety than this. The evocations of an incubation (sleeping in a shrine) are too many to ignore. Bethel, the name given the place in v. 19, had been a Canaanite shrine long before Israel entered the land. The ramp between earth and heaven is reminiscent of the ramp, or stairway up a Babylonian ziggurat, the tower shrine of the god standing beside the earthly temple in which men worshiped. "The gateway to heaven" recalls the gateway into a royal palace, and the angels coming and going evoke the messengers and emissaries of an earthly king. In light of the complex features of the E narrative, we seem to hear the author asserting that the divine king of all the earth revealed his activity to Jacob, an Israelite patriarch, when Jacob, fleeing for his life, faced an uncertain future.

E reports Jacob as having a vision, as seeing divine activity. J reports an audition (vv. 13-16). The scene has changed. The Lord is standing beside (rather than "above" as in RSV) Jacob, who is lying on the ground, presumably sleeping. Jacob is given the same promise of land and posterity earlier given Abraham (Gen. 13:14-17; 22:17) and Isaac (Gen. 26:4, 14). Even though he now is a fugitive, Jacob is assured that God's promise is so certain that he will protect Jacob while he is in an alien land and return him safely to the land he is to possess (v. 15). Jacob, awakening, acknowledges that the deity he had known in Beer-Sheba was God in this strange place also (v. 16).

The themes of J in vv. 13-16 are those which dominate all of this author's patriarchal narratives: the promises of land and progeny, and the transmission of those promises through all hazards. When vv. 13-16 are read in the context of the E story given them by the J editor, however, the result is a statement of the magnitude of the God making and guaranteeing the promises. It is the heavenly king, served by myriads of angels, who has covenanted with Israel.

Second Lesson: Rom. 5:1-11. In Rom. 5:1, the strongest ancient witnesses to the text read "let us have" (present subjunctive). Correctors of Sinaiticus and Vaticanus changed this to "we have" (present indicative). Translators of AV, AS, RSV, and a majority of commentators, have chosen the present indicative, apparently on theological grounds. The subjunctive is the more strongly attested reading and is followed here (with Moffatt, Goodspeed, NEB, and some commentators).

Rom. 5:1-11 is part of Paul's transition from his discussion of election by faith (1:16—4:25) to a consideration of the life of faith (6:1—8:39). Vv. 1-11 reflect the logical disorder sometimes found in lyrical outbursts. This exposition will attempt to deal with the thought of the passage rather more systematically than did the apostle, unfortunately at the price of a loss of power and beauty.

The concept upon which the whole rests is that we are judged righteous by God when we accept with faith the act of God in Christ. This act is described as Christ's voluntary death for sinners (vv. 6-8), an act contrasted by Paul with our reluctance to die even for a good man (the contrast between our unwillingness to die for a righteous man and our grudging willingness to die for a good man seems to be more a false start by Paul than a contrast of substance). We are not told here what "faith" means, whether it is mystical union with Christ, trust, or intellectual assent.

The effects of being justified through faith are three: we may now accept the peace of God, we may be allowed to share in his glory, and we know joy.

Paul appears to assert that we are given the choice to accept or to reject the peace of God (v. 1). The volitional element here echoes a like note in 2 Cor. 6:1 (the Second Lesson for Ash Wednesday). The phrase "the peace of God" is to be read in the light of Paul's Hellenistic-Jewish vocabulary. The Hebrew *shalom*, wholeness rather than the absence of strife, is likely to have been the meaning of "peace" for Paul. Since his Jewish heritage also was wholly theocentric, the phrase "the peace of God" would seem to have meant for Paul that wholeness, or completeness of life possible only when one stood in good relationship to God, the source of all life.

The second consequence of justification is the hope that we may "share in the glory of God" (v. 2). Paul's use of *doxa* (glory) was complex. We are told in v. 9 that we will be saved from "the wrath of God." Since we are also told that we already have experienced God's love (v. 5), the phrase "wrath of God" in v. 9 appears to be a reference to the final judgment. Those who escape the final judgment enter the eschatological kingdom, according to first century Jewish apocalyptic hope, in which the splendor of God's reign is complete. This could be described as his glory (cf. Isa. 40:5), and the saved who lived in that kingdom would share in his glory (cf. Isa. 43:7; 60:1-3).

The third consequence of justification is joy. This is the fruit of the knowledge of God's love given us by the Holy Spirit. Our knowledge enables us to endure adversity with equanimity and confidence since we are experiencing in the present the love of God which makes us confident of the future (vv. 3-5, 11).

Gospel: Mark 8:31-38. This passage falls into two parts: vv. 31-33 (Jesus teaching the disciples only) and vv. 34-38 (Jesus teaching both the disciples and a multitude).

Vv. 31-35 record one of the turning points in the dramatic structure of the Gospel of Mark. In response to Jesus' question about the popular reception of his ministry, Peter declared Jesus to be the Messiah (v. 29). From this point on, Jesus began to instruct his companions on the nature of his messianic vocation.

All of the evangelists consistently attribute the use of the term "Son of man" to Jesus and to him alone (14 times in Mark; 33 times in Matthew of which 14 are shared with Mark; 24 times in Luke of which 8 are shared with Mark and Matthew and 8 with Matthew only; 12 times in John). The title is used only once elsewhere in the NT (Acts 7:56). Although it is not clear in the Synoptic Gospels whether Jesus meant it to be applied as a messianic title to himself or to another than himself, it is clear that the early church remembered Jesus' frequent use of it. Thus we have reason to believe that these verses contain a reliable memory of Jesus' ministry even though v. 31 is in indirect discourse.

A suffering Messiah was not unknown in Judaism (cf. Isa. 52:13–53:12), and the final outcome of the consistent animus of Jewish leaders to Jesus' ministry (Mark 2:6 f., 16; 3:6, 22, etc.) may already have become clear to him. The prominence of the figure of the triumphant, even regal, Messiah in first century Jewish hopes, however, may still have dominated Peter's expectations for Jesus. Whatever the reason, he took Jesus aside to protest his predictions of his death (v. 32).

Jesus rejected Peter's protest before the whole company (v. 33). The reproof seems strangely harsh. Peter is addressed as Satan in a command echoing Matt. 4:10, and the inference is that Peter's protest was a temptation to Jesus as strong as those offered by Satan in the wilderness. Peter had advocated something other than God's will as Jesus had come to know it. Nevertheless, Peter was a close follower, one already able to recognize Jesus to be the Messiah. Was Peter's being "on man's side," having let his affection for Jesus blind him to God's will? If this be correct, this is a difficult teaching!

Vv. 34-38 preserve three sayings. Each is reported twice in Matthew and Luke (Mark 8:34 = Matt. 16:24; 10:38; Luke 9:23; 14:27; Mark 8:35-37 = Matt. 16:25 f.; 10:39; Luke 9:24 f.; 17:33; Mark 8:38 = Matt. 16:27; 10:33; Luke 9:26; 12:9). This attests to the strength of the tradition that these were Jesus' sayings, but it also suggests that the circumstance in which they originally had been spoken had been lost. A comparison of each saying with its parellels further indicates that the precise wording of each was uncertain. Thus we would be well advised to concentrate on the primary thrust of each rather than on its details.

In v. 34, we are commanded to serve Christ and his gospel with such devotion that we will risk death for him. Crucifixion was a well-known form of execution, and the condemned often was forced to carry his own cross. Bearing a cross in this passage, therefore, is accepting the risk of death for the sake of Christ, not bearing the misfortunes of life with fortitude (even though that is admirable in itself).

Vv. 35-37 describe the primacy of the decision to be for or against

Christ. NT writers consistently affirm Jesus to be "the way, the truth, and the life" (John 14:6). He who denied being a follower of Christ when interrogated during persecution might survive physically, yet he would lose the life given through Christ. We should remember, when reading this, Papias' report that the Gospel of Mark was written in Rome by a companion of Peter after his martyrdom.

The title "Son of man" appears again in v. 38 in a way which underscores the problem of the identity of this figure. Is Jesus distinguishing here between himself and the Son of man, is he speaking of himself as the Son of man at that future time when he was to come again, or is the early church here affirming its belief that Jesus either was, or would become the Son of man? We cannot now decide with complete confidence which (if any) of these is correct. V. 38 is an apocalyptic statement of the theme of vv. 35-37. Those who repudiate Jesus now will be repudiated by the Son of man when he comes in the full panoply of his power at the end of this age. Only here and in Jesus' prayer in the Garden of Gethsemane (Mark 14:36) does this evangelist use "father" as a term for God.

HOMILETICAL INTERPRETATION

At the center of the biblical message is the good news that God is a God of gracious love. The gods of philosophy are supreme beings who remain clothed in awesome secrecy. Some truth about them may be discovered by a few great thinkers who probe the secrets of the heavens but to the rest of humanity they are unknown entities. The biblical God is not one who waits for human beings to discover him. On the contrary, he takes the initiative and seeks his people. He chooses the Jewish people that through them he might approach all peoples. Before ever we thought of seeking God he was seeking us. Jesus said to his disciples, "You did not choose me, but I chose you . . ." (John 15:16). Those words can be used to sum up the relationship between God and his people throughout the Bible.

God's gracious love means that God seeks us, but it also means that God receives and forgives sinful human beings. The popular view of religion always pictures God as the great judge in the sky. His heavenly computer is keeping a daily record of everyone's good and bad deeds. When the time of judgment comes those whose score of good deeds outweighs their score of evil deeds will be accepted and rewarded by God. But those whose evil deeds weigh more heavily will be cast into punishment. The biblical God, however, breaks radically from this popular picture. He accepts not only the good people but he seeks the sinful and the outcast. He is a God who desires to save rather than to destroy or punish.

The gracious love of God comes out clearly in both the First and Second Lessons for this Sunday. Jacob is fleeing from the justifiable wrath of his brother. To this point in his life Jacob has proven himself to be a scheming cheat who has misled his aged father and stolen his brother's birthright and blessing. As time passes he will add still further sharp practices to his record. It seems unlikely that God would choose such an unsavory character as Jacob for his purposes. But the whole point of this passage is that God comes to the renegade Jacob and renews with him the covenant made with Abraham, his grandfather. Jacob is promised that he is to be the one through whom the covenant will be transmitted to the coming generations. "For I will not leave you until I have done that of which I have spoken to you" (v. 15). Jacob has not proven himself to be particularly trustworthy, but God pledges to Jacob his trustworthiness.

The Second Lesson is a beautiful rendition of the same theme. As God came with promise to the scheming Jacob, so Paul tells us Jesus came to die for sinful humanity. "But God shows his love for us in that while we were yet sinners Christ died for us" (v. 8). This is startling news! As Paul sees, most of us would be reluctant to give our lives for a righteous person. How can we comprehend one who so willingly gave his life for all of the unrighteous ones? But this is the nature of God's love. He does not love us insofar as we have acted to deserve it. On the contrary, he loves us in our sin and seeks to deliver us from our sinful state. And so, as Jacob received God's promise and blessings despite his sinful state, Paul assures us that in Christ we are blessed. We have been reconciled to God so that we may accept the peace of God, share in God's glory, and know joy. (See exegesis.)

At first sight the Gospel reading does not seem to fit in with the theme of the First and Second Lessons. As the exegesis points out, it seems unduly harsh when Jesus calls Peter "Satan." We must read this passage in light of its context within Mark's Gospel. Peter has just made his epochal confession "You are the Christ" (Mark 8:29). No doubt, in the minds of the disciples there had been the hope or even the belief that Jesus was God's promised Christ. But none had dared to speak the hidden hope until Peter blurted it out. According to Matthew's version of the same story, Jesus told Peter that his words had been a revelation from God and hence Peter would be the rock upon which the church would be built (Matt. 16:13-20). All of this meant, of course, that the disciples would see Jesus as the one in whom God's covenant with his people would be fulfilled.

The passage for this Sunday follows immediately after Peter's confession. Jesus began to teach his followers that the Son of man must

The Second Sunday in Lent

suffer, be rejected by the religious and political authorities, and be put to death. This teaching is similar to Paul's words in today's Second Lesson. Christ has come to give his life for a sinful humanity. But the words must have sounded strange and dismaying to the disciples. Obviously they were not prepared to find that God's Christ would come as a suffering servant. Probably, like most people in their time, they were hoping for a conquering-hero type of Messiah, one who would bring victory over the foes of his people. And so it was Peter who again spoke out the thoughts that were in the minds of all the disciples. He rebuked Jesus' view that the Christ should suffer and die. This rebuke brought upon him Jesus' stern words "Get behind me, Satan! For you are not on the side of God, but of men" (v. 33).

Jesus probably calls Peter "Satan" for two reasons. In the first place, Peter has failed to see God's basic purpose. Peter is speaking "for men" in that he is expressing the presuppositions of the world that God and his Christ will come on behalf of the good people. To the good, Christ will give his rewards. Peter could not yet understand the gracious love that would die for sinful people. But perhaps even more important, Jesus calls Peter Satan because Jesus hears the temptation of Satan coming through Peter's words. In Gethsemane Jesus was to pray in agony as he sought to have the cup of suffering taken from him. Our temptations are always most difficult when they come to us from our friends. It is not too difficult to resist the temptation that comes from one that we despise. Upon such a one's lips the temptation appears in all of its loathsomeness. But when the friend expresses the same thing, it suddenly appears harmless, nay, it even seems good because it becomes part of our relationship with our friend.

Jesus' words to Peter may be harsh. They rebuked the ideas that Peter was expressing. But it is important to see that they were not a rejection of Peter himself. On the contrary, in the next chapter Mark reports that Jesus took Peter along with James and John to witness his transfiguration. Jesus, who gave his life for sinners, would not cast away from him a disciple even when he became a voice of Satan.

The concluding verses in the Gospel reading can be seen as Jesus' advice on how we ought to respond to God's gracious love. God has given himself totally for us in his grace and so Jesus calls us to give ourselves totally to God. Because Christ has taken up his cross for us, we are called to take up our cross for him. God's grace comes to us freely. We do not earn it, deserve it, or in any way receive it as our right. But it is not, in Bonhoeffer's phrase, a "cheap grace." When God's love lays hold upon us we find that we are changed. Because we have been loved by God we love God in turn and thus we love those whom God loves, our neighbors. When we love someone, we are prepared to give ourselves in costly service to them.

In v. 35 Jesus speaks paradoxically by saying that those who seek to save their lives will lose them while those who are ready to lose their lives for Jesus' cause will find them. The paradox brings out the nature of responding to God's grace. In our natural state we are all self-centered and thus we naturally seek salvation for ourselves. Because we think that God is like we are, we assume that to get God on our side and to win salvation we must do things which will please and flatter him. And so we use God for our own ends. This self-centered determination to advance and save ourselves, says Jesus, ends up in alienating ourselves from both God and ourselves. Our dedication to save our lives destroys them. But when God's gracious love takes hold of us we are literally pulled outside of ourselves. Whenever we love we do tend to forget ourselves and seek to please the loved one. When we experience God's gracious love we are won to love in return and in the love for God we quit worrying about ourselves, our salvation, our interests. We are prepared to give our lives to God and the strange wonder is that it is in such a giving up of the self that we begin for the first time to experience true selfhood.

Taken together, our three readings for this Sunday describe the essence of justification by grace through faith. In the Old Testament reading we see the forgiving love of God that pursues even the shifty sinner, Jacob. In the Second Lesson we learn of how God's son died for the enemies of God that they might be reconciled to the God against whom they had rebelled. In the Gospel we are invited to respond to God's gracious love with a responding love whereby we give ourselves to the God who has first given himself to us.

The Third Sunday in Lent

Lutheran	Roman Catholic	Episcopal	Pres./UCC/Chr.	Methodist/COCU
Exod. 20:1-17	Exod. 20:1-17	Exod. 3:1-8b, 10-15	Exod. 20:1-3, 7-8, 12-17	Exod. 20:1-17
Rom. 10:5-13	1 Cor. 1:22-25	Eph. 5:8-14	1 Cor. 1:22-25	1 Cor. 1:22-25
John 2:13-22	John 2:13-25	John 3:14-21	John 4:19-26	John 2:13-22

EXEGESIS

First Lesson: Exod. 20:1-17. The Ten Commandments in Exod. 20:1-17 (found also, with a few important variations, in Deut. 5:6-21) are unconditional demands or prohibitions. They are called apodictic (i.e., absolute) laws. They had a long history before reaching their present form. The brevity of vv. 3, 13-16 contrasts sharply with the explanatory or hortatory expansions in vv. 4-12, 17. This, and the differences between Exod. 20:1-17 and Deut. 5:6-21 suggest that all of the laws originally were brief. The expansions may have arisen as the circumstances of life changed or in response to major shifts in worship (e.g., from emphasis on God acting in the exodus [Deut. 5:15] to God acting in creation [Exod. 20:11]). No date or origin can be given the commandments in their original form. All of the evidence used in discussions of these questions is taken from the later expansions of the original, brief commandments.

The laws are identified in v. 1 as "the words of God." In Deut. 4:13, they are called "the Ten Words" (whence our decalogue). V. 2 gives the basis of the Lord's right to make demands of Israel. The declaration "I am Yahweh your God" is a covenantal title, and it recalls the self-designation used by Hittite emperors in treaties with vassals. In those treaties, the emperor's right to the vassal's obedience had been won in battle, and the victory was always reported in the treaty. The similar element here is the reference to the Lord's display of compassionate might in delivering Israel from slavery. Just as the Hittite treaty included a list of the forms of obedience demanded of the vassal, so here also the will of God for Israel is described in the commandments which follow (vv. 3-17).

V. 3 prohibits bringing other gods into the presence of the Lord, although it does not deny their existence. Vv. 4-6 prohibit the worship ("you shall not bow down") of a representation of any god. The deity in the waters under the earth (the abyss) may be the god of chaos in the Semitic creation myth: Rahab, Leviathan, or The Serpent (cf. Isa. 27:1;

51:9; Ps. 89:10; Job 26:12 f., etc.). Because the Lord was jealous of his right to Israel's allegiance, he would hold an entire household (which might include four generations) guilty for apostasy. His love, however, was greater than his anger and would flow out to a large number of those related to the faithful. Since the name was believed to contain a person's essence, v. 7 prohibits violating the Lord's sovereignty by using his name for any false reason (i.e., for a reason desired by man—including witchcraft and false witness—rather than those commanded by God). Vv. 8-11 prescribe Sabbath observance. In biblical Hebrew, "to remember" includes acting upon a recollection. That which was holy was set apart from the common. Therefore a holy day was lived differently than other days. On the Sabbath, all of the household was to stop work because God rested after creation (cf. Gen. 2:1-3; P. Deut. 5:12-15 bases Sabbath observance on the exodus).

The Ten Words conclude with six commandments governing human relationships. Honoring authority of parents (who ruled the family until they were quite old) is commanded (v. 12). Unauthorized killing (excluding judicial execution and killing in war, acts for which different verbs were used), adultery, theft, and the corruption of the judicial process by giving false testimony are banned. The list ends with a prohibition of desiring strongly to possess all that belongs to another (v. 17). "House" here seems to mean "household" since what follows constitutes the household (with the wife given the place of honor).

Second Lesson: Rom. 10:5-13. In Rom. 10:5-13, Paul uses free quotations from Lev. 18:5 (v. 5), Deut. 30:11-14 (vv. 6-8), Isa. 28:16 (v. 11), and Joel 2:32 (v. 32) as part of his argument that all those, whether Jew or Gentile, who accept Christ will be counted righteous by God. Since Paul's ways of expounding Scripture differ so sharply from the methods of modern critical exegesis, the force of his argument here can be described only when the context in which he wrote is understood.

The OT Lesson for today makes it clear that ancient Israel viewed the law as a statement of the will of the God who had established his sovereignty by an act of compassion. Thus the basis for obedience was responding to the divine act in love. The God acting in the exodus was Yahweh, translated in the Septuagint used by Paul as *kurios*. Early Christians called Christ *kurios* (lord, master), and God was affirmed as acting to save men in the ministry, death, and resurrection of Christ. Thus Paul had both a linguistic and a functional basis for equating what Yahweh had done for Israel and what Christ had done (and was doing) for Christians. As a result,

Paul applied Joel 2:32, originally said about Yahweh, to Christ as *kurios* and to all who can affirm Christ to be *kurios*.

When these aspects of Paul's thought are kept in mind, it becomes clear that his use of Deut. 30:11-14—even though it is a commentary, or midrash, formed by explanatory interpolations—does justice to the basic viewpoint of Deuteronomy. Paul is contrasting righteousness achieved by the performance of all of the law—said to be possible (v. 5) on the basis of Lev. 18:5—with the righteousness of faith in Christ by which the Christian lives. To defend the latter, he quoted phrases excerpted from the Greek text of Deut. 30:11-14, interspersing explanations of what he believed the phrases being quoted to mean for Christians. It is not an exegetical method in good standing today, yet Paul did express by means of it the basic Deuteronomic insistence that God saved Israel because of his grace and not Israel's merit (Deut. 7:6-8; 8:17; 9:4).

Paul's interpretations, when read in the light of the material quoted from Deuteronomy, are significant. Men could not hasten the coming of the Messiah by their devotion to the law (they cannot "ascend into heaven" to bring the Messiah down)—some Jews held that the Messiah or the new age would come when the law had been perfectly obeyed (2 Baruch 15:7; 44:7-14; Jubilees 23:16 f.)—because he had already come. Nor did they need to seek the Messiah in Sheol (descending into the abyss to raise Christ from the dead) because he is already raised from the dead. As a living, present reality, he is as close to them as the lips with which they confess him to be Lord.

Paul's Jewish heritage encouraged him to understand that there was an integral relationship between the inner person and what the person says. Both had to affirm the act of God in Christ (vv. 9 f.). All who do this, whether Jew or Gentile, will be saved (vv. 11-13). Since Paul here again speaks of a future salvation in addition to the present knowledge of the love of God (Rom. 5:5), the salvation of v. 13 is probably eschatological.

Gospel: John 2:13-22. John 2:13-22 contains the Johannine report of traditions recorded in different contexts and words in the Synoptic Gospels. The story of the cleansing of the temple in Mark 11:15-17 (Matt. 21:12 f.; Luke 19:45 f.) is placed early in Passion Week. Here, it comes early in Jesus' ministry. In Mark 11:17, Jesus protests the dishonesty of the merchants in the temple (echoing Jer. 7:11). In John 2:16, Jesus protests any commerce there (possibly recalling Zech. 14:21). The Markan account ends with the Jewish authorities reacting to the cleansing by plotting Jesus' death (v. 18). John concludes with the Jewish leaders' challenge of the basis of Jesus' authority and with a discussion of the destruction and rebuilding of the temple. A similar challenge is reported in Mark 11:27-33 as happening on a different day and for a different reason, and a prediction of the destruction of the temple is recorded in Mark 14:58 as part of the false witness against Jesus during his trial.

In all of this, we seem to be faced with different uses of early Christian traditions. The Synoptic Gospels appear to be somewhat the more historical. It is unlikely that the rulers in Jerusalem would let a direct challenge to essential services in the temple to go unheeded for two years. This conclusion does not deny Johannine use of early traditions. It does encourage us to find the theological content being conveyed by the fourth evangelist in his arrangements and reporting of his sources.

Writing for Greek Christians aware of themselves as non-Jewish, the evangelist may also be distinguishing between a Jewish and a Christian passover ("the passover of the Jews," v. 13; cf. 1 Cor. 5:7). The sale of animals for sacrifice and the exchange of coins unlawful for use in paying the temple tax because they displayed a human likeness were a convenience to worshipers coming from a distance (v. 14). These businesses were carried on in the temple court (*hieron*). Jesus expelled the tradesmen because any commerce there was improper (vv. 15 f.). This may have been an attack on the whole of the temple cult since both sacrifices and the support of the temple through payment of the tax were made more difficult. The phrase "my Father's house" rather than "our Father's house" implies a special relationship between Jesus and God, and it may have been a messianic claim.

The Jewish response was to ask for proof of Jesus' authority (v. 18; cp. 2 Kings 19:29; Isa. 7:10-16). Jesus replied, in effect, "If you want a sign strongly enough to destroy the temple (*naos* here rather than *hieron*), I will give it to you by rebuilding the temple in three days."

The evangelist has expanded his sources in vv. 17, 20-23. In v. 17, Ps. 69:9 is quoted from the Septuagint in a retrospect gaining its force by changing the past tense in the psalm to a future tense. The disciples are thus reported as realizing that Jesus' zeal for a proper use of the temple caused his death. In this, v. 17 echoes Mark 11:18. V. 20 is a literary device used in Hellenistic literature (and often in the Fourth Gospel) to set the stage for a clarification of meaning—here the explanation that the temple to be raised up is Jesus' body (v. 21). The forty-seven years' building time for the temple reported in v. 20 has created more problems than it has solved. According to Josephus (Antiquities XV, xi. 1), Herod the Great began the building in 20/19 B.C. It was not completed until A.D.

63. The obscurity is deepened by the comment in John 8:57 that Jesus was not yet fifty. It may be that the evangelist had no interest in, or knowledge of, the precise chronology of the building of the temple. V. 22 records how the disciples remembered Jesus' statement about rebuilding the temple after the resurrection, recognizing at the same time the messianic significance of Ps. 69:9 (cited in v. 17), and "believed" both.

If it be concluded that the fourth evangelist recast received traditions to convey a message in his narrative, his meaning should be sought in the narrative as it now stands. In John 2:13-22, the message seems to be the presentation of Jesus as the Messiah. Devotion to him would replace the Jewish temple cult. It was this threat that aroused the implacable opposition of those responsible for that cult, and it was the acceptance of such a messiahship that constituted the disciples' post-resurrection belief.

HOMILETICAL INTERPRETATION

The Ten Commandments are often referred to as the basic ethical code for all human life. As such the Ten Commandments are seen as the Judaeo-Christian version of the ethical principles that are universally accepted by the human race. This is partly true. The last six of the commandments (vv. 12-17) are most certainly not unique to Jews and Christians. All peoples extol the honoring of parents. Some, such as the Chinese, have put even greater emphasis upon this than Jews and Christians do. All societies prohibit murder, adultery, stealing, and false witness against neighbors. Coveting of the neighbor's possessions is discouraged in all societies. Certainly this group of commandments is known to people quite apart from biblical revelation. It would be difficult to find a society anywhere that did not extol or enforce these ethical ideals.

When we turn, however, to vv. 1-8 we find a framework for all of the commandments that gives a uniqueness to the Judaeo-Christian statement. We are told that God spoke and identified himself as "the Lord your God, who brought you out of the land of Egypt, out of the house of bondage." The ethical commandments are thus put into the framework of the relationship of the people with their God who, having made his covenant with them, delivered them from bondage in Egypt. The commandments are not orders sent down from on high by the ruler of the universe, they are part of the covenant relationship between God and the people whom he has chosen and loved.

And because the Lord who brought them out of Egypt is speaking, his first commandment is: "You shall have no other gods before me" (v. 3).

The second commandment (v. 4) is really just an expansion of the first. If the people are to have no gods before their Lord, then they should not make graven images. At first sight these two commandments do not seem particularly difficult for modern man. We are a monotheistic culture and we agree that the one God is the God of Judaism and Christianity. In the ancient world a person had a choice between a vast number of gods. But in North America it would appear that we have only a choice between atheism and the one God. Even when other religions are brought to our continent, the gods of such religions are usually identified with our God. Furthermore, it would not seem that we are tempted today to make graven images because that is not the way any religion operates in our culture. A typical joke tells of a man who listens to a fiery sermon on the Ten Commandments. As he leaves the church he says to his wife, "Well, at least I have not made any graven images." The point of the joke lies in the assumption that graven images are irrelevant in our culture.

But a second look quickly shows that the first two commandments are far from irrelevant. Paul Tillich described faith as "being ultimately concerned." In life we are concerned with many things and some concerns are obviously more important to us than others. We are concerned to save money but that concern is not as important to most of us as caring adequately for our families. The concern for the family thus proves more ultimate than the concern to increase our savings. Life consists, therefore, of continually weighing our priorities and deciding which concerns should take precedence. Tillich's point is that a religious faith is an ultimate concern, a concern that takes priority over all other concerns. It is Tillich's philosophical translation of Jesus' words about loving God with all our heart and soul and mind (Matt. 22:37). In light of this, the first two commandments are asking us whether God is our ultimate concern. A graven image is not something that we carve out with our hands, a graven image is a concern which we allow to take priority over God. Idolatry, said Tillich, consists of giving our ultimate allegiance and concern to that which is not ultimate. By that standard we are not as innocent of disobeying the first two commandments as we would like to think. We have been created to have God at the center of our lives but we have allowed a host of concerns to push God to the periphery of life. That is having other gods before him. It is the modern way of making graven images.

The third commandment (v. 7) prohibits taking God's name in vain. This follows from all that has been said. Because God has entered into covenant with his people, because he has kept his promise and delivered them from bondage, the relationship between God and his people is a serious one. Therefore, they should not take the name of God lightly or thoughtlessly. Such a use of God would be a denial of their relationship to him. The problem here is that all too often we assume that this is simply a prohibition of what we call cursing or swearing. Actually the third commandment probably has little to do with most forms of cursing and swearing in today's world. The man who lightly tosses off "god-damns" or uses Jesus' name as an expletive is not really taking the *Lord's* name in vain. He has not stopped to think what his words mean, they are but a part of the thoughtless vocabulary that he has inherited.

Much more serious than the mindless swearing or cursing of the modern age is the tendency of believers to use God's name to bless their many personal causes and concerns. The truly blasphemous taking of God's name in vain is that which uses God and the Bible to justify racial discrimination, aggressive war, and a host of other things that are contrary to God's revelation in Christ.

The fourth commandment (v. 8) calls the people to "remember the sabbath day." As God rested, so his people are to have rest. Because God has entered into the covenant relationship with his people it is important to have set aside a time and place where the relationship is remembered and where it is renewed. In the service of worship, as the community hears God's word and speaks their words to God, the covenant relationship is renewed.

The Ten Commandments are a vivid reminder that the covenant between God and his people is a two-way agreement. God took the initiative to form the covenant, he pledged himself to his people and bestowed upon them his many blessings. And then he called them to respond to his initiative by living as the people of the covenant. The story of the OT, however, is the story of the people's failure to keep their covenant. When we turn to the Second Lesson for the day we find that it is written from the perspective of the new covenant that has been made by God in Christ. Paul is contrasting the righteousness of faith with the righteousness based on law. God gave his law to the people whom he had chosen and delivered in order that the relationship between himself and his people might be continued. But the people used the law to exalt themselves rather than to glorify God. When that happens people dream that they might "ascend into heaven." (See exegesis.) And so it is that people continually think that if they can just live the good life they will solve all problems. If we can just get a bit more of the right technology, if we can just get the right economic system working, if we can just have less governmental action or if we can just have more governmental action, then we shall have solved the problems that beset us. But no matter how fine the methods we assemble or how proficient we become in using them, so long as people are self-centered the good methods are used again to try and "ascend into heaven." We are more concerned to exalt ourselves than to serve God.

In describing the righteousness of faith, Paul says, "if you confess with your lips that Jesus is Lord and believe in your heart that God raised him from the dead, you will be saved" (v. 9). It is interesting that he links confessing with the lips to believing with the heart. The righteousness of faith is not just a matter of saying the right things when stimulated in the correct way. A person may affirm a host of orthodox doctrines and not really have faith at all. Nonetheless, Paul seems to be saying that verbal confession is an important part of faith. Where there is faith it has the desire to make itself known and to share the good news it has heard through confession with the lips. Such confession will be an effective witness, however, only if the speaker also believes in his or her heart. To believe in the heart is to have the ultimate concern that we discussed in connection with the OT Lesson.

At first sight it is not clear just how the Gospel should be related to the First and Second Lessons for the day. The exegesis concludes, however, that John has used this story in order to present Jesus as the Messiah. His coming has meant the replacement of the temple cult which represented the old covenant. So interpreted, we can see the three readings for the day blending together.

The OT Lesson consists of the center of the law that God gave to his people. Laws, such as the Ten Commandments, can be seen in two ways. They can be seen as a response of the covenant people to their God. Because God has delivered his people, the people desire to know what they can do to please God who has done so much for them. But such laws can also be seen, as the Second Lesson makes clear, as a way whereby people exalt themselves and storm heaven. The laws are no longer seen as a way of continuing what God has started and as an expression of love to God who first loved us. Instead, they are seen as a means whereby we can exalt ourselves, win favor with God, and earn our place in the universe. Given the first view, the laws are an expression of the people's unity with God. Given the second view the laws are an expression of the division between the people and God. In the first view the laws are a means of communication with God, in the second they are barriers to be hurdled if the people are to come to God.

Where the laws are seen as a barrier to be overcome, it is inevitable that worship itself will be commercialized. The keeping of the sabbath, worship, and obedience to God, are no longer precious opportunities to express fellowship with God, they become tasks to perform in order to earn God's pleasure. The father's house becomes "a house of trade" (John 2:16). Since it is the place where we try to buy our way to God, it does not seem out of place to do other business there. And so we have the temple in Jesus' day with livestock and birds being sold and coins being exchanged. In cleansing the temple, John is saying to us, Jesus was doing more than chastising the villains on the spot. He was introducing a new order. In his messianic claim he was bringing to an end the whole idea of buying our way to God with good deeds. So understood, the Gospel for the day calls us to see how Jesus, in his life, death, and resurrection has freed us to be in the true covenant relationship with God.

The Fourth Sunday in Lent

Lutheran	Roman Catholic	Episcopal	Pres./UCC/Chr.	Methodist/COCU
Num. 21:4-9	2 Chron. 36:14-16, 19-23	Exod. 16:2-8, 13-15	2 Chron. 36:14-21	2 Chron. 36:14-21
Eph. 2:4-10	Eph. 2:4-10	Gal. 4:26-5:1	Eph. 2:1-10	Eph. 2:1-10
John 3:14-21	John 3:14-21	Mark 8:12-21	John 3:14-21	John 3:14-21

EXEGESIS

First Lesson: Num. 21:4-9. This is one of several passages in the OT which describes Israel as complaining during the wilderness wanderings (cf. Exod. 14:10-12; 16:1-31; Num. 11:1-34; 20:2-13; Psalm 78; Ezek. 20:5-26, etc.). The narrative is introduced by a note which describes tersely the Israelites as retracing their steps from Mount Hor (where they had stopped according to Num. 20:22-29: P) southward to the Sea of Reeds (*Yam Suph*; cf. Exod. 13:18) in order to detour around Edom. The Edomites had prohibited the Israelites from passing through their land (Num. 20:14-21).

As the Israelites moved back into the desert, they became testy (lit: short of *nephesh*: v. 4), and their complaints swiftly became a reproach against God and Moses for leading them out of the security of Egypt into the perils of the wilderness. The exodus is the divine act in the OT upon which the Lord's sovereignty over Israel is primarily based. Speaking against the guidance of God in the exodus was a serious denial of his sovereignty. The Lord's response was to send fiery serpents among the people which caused widespread death (v. 6).

The serpents are called *nehashim seraphim* in v. 6, *nahash* (serpent) alone in v. 7, and *seraph* (fiery) alone in v. 8. *Nahash* is used throughout v. 9. The fiery serpents, or the fiery ones of vv. 6 and 8 call to mind the *seraphim* of Isa. 6:2, 6 where one of them is the agency through which Isaiah is cleansed of his sin. The bronze serpent mentioned twice in v. 9 recalls Nehushtan, the bronze serpent worshiped in the temple in Jerusalem as late as the reign of Hezekiah (2 Kings 18:4).

The danger created by the serpents caused the people to recognize their grumbling to be rebellion against God and against Moses, his representative. They repented (v. 7), and Moses prayed to God on their behalf. Their request that the serpents be removed was not granted. Instead, Moses was commanded to make a likeness of the fiery ones to put in a prominent place. Those who looked at it when bitten would survive.

The Fourth Sunday in Lent

This narrative had a tangled history, little of which we can reconstruct now with confidence. Ps. 78:67-72 and Ezek. 20:5-26 suggest that the motif of revolt against God's guidance in the wilderness was a Jerusalem, or Zion tradition (Ezekiel had been a priest in Jerusalem before becoming a prophet in the exile). It may be more than coincidence that a figure of a "fiery one" was an agent for God in the call of Isaiah, a Jerusalemite (Isa. 6:2, 6), just as an image of a "fiery one" was the agent of God's salvation in Num. 21:9. A naturalistic interpretation would reject the pattern of cultic traditions just outlined. It would identify the *seraphim* as poisonous reptiles whose bites caused inflammation. The story could then be judged to be the report of a memory of a crisis in the wilderness during which snake bites were treated either by the kind of sympathetic magic described in 1 Sam. 6:1-16 or by recourse to one of the healing cults associated with snakes which were so common in Semitic antiquity. The primary point of the story as it now stands is clear. God provided the means for the healing of his people from the ravages caused by their sin after they had repented.

Second Lesson: Eph. 2:4-10. Paul is identified as the author of Ephesians in 1:1 (and 3:1). The earliest confirmation of this appears in Marcion's "canon" (A.D. 140-160). There are strong reasons to question Pauline authorship, however: the frequent parallels to phrases found elsewhere in the Pauline corpus suggest quotations from Paul by another writer; the elevation of the "holy apostles" as the founders of the church (2:20) contrasts with Paul's occasionally jaundiced view of them (2 Cor. 11:5; 12:11); views stated here contrast with those found in Paul (cf. vv. 5 f., 10 here below); and there is a vocabulary of about 100 words unique to this letter. The view is held here that the letter reflects a response to Paul's epistles. The author's identity is unknown, as also is the audience to which he was writing since the phrase "who are at Ephesus" is lacking from 1:1 in Codex Sinaiticus and Codex Vaticanus (and thus from modern translations).

Our passage opens with the affirmation that God has restored us to life because of the immensity of his love for us, even though we had died because of our sins (2:1-3) by making us to share in Christ's life (vv. 4 f.). V. 5 concludes with a terse recapitulation of this theme. Paul had written often of life "in Christ" (cf. Gal. 2:20; Phil. 3:10 f.; Rom. 6:1-11, etc.), always affirming that such life included being crucified with Christ. That is lacking here.

V. 6 describes the Christian as united with the risen Christ seated on his heavenly throne (cf. 1:20). The verbs here (and in v. 5), compounded with *syn* (with), "alive together," "raised up with," and "sit with," are all aorists. God has already done these things. The Christian is enthroned now beside Christ (a statement not found in other letters usually judged to have been written by Paul). The phrase "in the heavenly places" is applied to the risen Christ (1:20), to people living in this life (2:6), and to supernatural powers (3:10), suggesting that it describes a state of existence before God rather than life in either a future or supramundane realm. V. 7 extends God's display of love toward us into the future. The phrase "the coming ages," which normally in the NT refers to the age after the return of Christ, seems here simply to designate an indefinite future.

Vv. 8 f. return to the theme of the divine initiative in our salvation. When "faith" is defined as belief, we can will ourselves to believe and thus achieve for ourselves the faith by means of which God saves us. V. 8 rejects this possibility. "Faith" itself is given by God. "Trust" (with NEB) thus is a good translation for *pistis* here. All good works enable us to magnify ourselves (v. 9) and thereby diminish the love of God which redeems us precisely when we do not merit it.

V. 10 is striking. The redeemed have been created by God in order to do the good deeds he has prepared. Thus, even though trust in God's love is not divorced from conduct, conduct is as much foreordained by God as is salvation. This contrasts markedly with the responsibility Paul imposes upon the saved (as in Gal. 6:10; Col. 1:10, and, implicitly, in his instructions about conduct throughout his letters).

Gospel: John 3:14-21. The problem of the authorship of sayings attributed to Jesus in the Fourth Gospel is acute in John 3:14-21. These verses seem to be part of Jesus' reply to Nicodemus, yet the shift from the first person singular to first person plural in v. 11, the consistent use of the third person when speaking of the Son of man or the Son (clearly identified as Jesus in this Gospel) in vv. 13-21, and the impression of a post-resurrection perspective throughout encourage the conclusion that this passage is a statement by the evangelist. It will be so treated here.

V. 14 draws a parallel between the elevation of the bronze serpent by Moses (Num. 21:8 f.) and the elevation (*hypsoun*) of Jesus, both of which had salvific results. *Hypsoun* refers to being lifted up upon the cross in John 8:28, but it is used to describe the ascension in Acts 2:33 and 5:31. The Johannine usage of the verb, especially in the light of John 12:32, may include both the resurrection and the ascension. The parallel to Num. 21:8 f. is in the act of being elevated. The serpent is not a "type" for Christ or for his work (as in Barnabas 12:5-7 or in Tertullian, *Against*

Marcion iii 18, where the pole on which the serpent was fastened is a type for the cross). The "eternal life" of vv. 15 f. that is given those who believe in the Son is a quality of existence available now. It is the Johannine equivalent to the term "kingdom of God" in the Synoptic Gospels. It is life lived fully in accordance with God's will and thus as he had created it to be lived. Death was held to be an intrusion into life as intended by God (Paul's statements in 1 Cor. 15:21 f. and Rom. 5:12 are so terse and categorical that they seem to be quotations of widely known Christian aphorisms). Life without end would thus be a part of "eternal life," but only one aspect of it.

V. 16, probably the best known and loved verse in Scripture, opens an exposition of vv. 14 f. in which the themes of the love of God and judgment are intertwined. The verb *agapao* (to love) is used in the Fourth Gospel to describe God's relationship to man (cf. 14:23; 17:23). It is not so used in the Synoptics. The object of the love of God in 3:16 is "the world" which had been created by God through the *logos* (John 1:10). Elsewhere in this Gospel, God is said to love only those who love his Son (John 14:21, 23; 17:23) or, of course, the Son (John 10:17, etc.). The words used in v. 16 to describe God's relationship with his Son recall the story of the sacrifice of Isaac (Gen. 22:2; Tertullian, *Against Marcion* iii 18 declared that Isaac bearing the wood for his own sacrifice was a type of Christ bearing his cross). In both passages, the magnitude of the sacrifice is described by portraying the closeness of the relationship between the father and the son to be killed. Abraham was not divine, but human analogy is used often in Scripture to describe the ineffable God.

God acted because of his love. Therefore his purpose was to save, not to judge (v. 17). The outpouring of divine love was on such a scale, however, that the decision to accept or to reject it is an ultimate decision. Thus God's act of love becomes the occasion for judgment. Those who believe in the gift given in the Son escape condemnation and receive eternal life. Those who reject the Son condemn themselves.

To "believe in him" (vv. 15 f.) seems to be both to share the experience of the presence of the risen Christ and to assent to propositions about him. Those who experience the risen Christ have already entered into the eternal life where the elevated Christ now is.

The description of judgment in vv. 18b-20 is consistent with statements elsewhere in the Gospel. God has turned over the role of judge to his Son (5:22, 27), and the Son's judgments are just (5:30; 8:16). Yet men judge themselves by their response to the Son (12:47 f.). "To judge," especially in Semitic antiquity, included establishing the facts, determining standing before the law, pronouncing sentence, and executing it (cf. Jer. 26:7-19, 24). The Son embodies man's true life before God. Belief in him enables Christians to enter into it. Who, then, has judged those who reject the Son and close off eternal life for themselves?

The polarities of light versus darkness, and doing good versus doing wickedness (vv. 19 f.)—found also in the Dead Sea Scrolls (Manual of Discipline ii, iv)—clarify further the nature of the choice to accept or to reject the Son of man. Those who do wickedness love wickedness. They shun the light that created the world as the *logos* which has returned as the Son (John 1:1-5, 10). Those who "do the truth" (v. 21) come to the light, the source of the truth (cf. 1:4, 9), that their deeds of truth may be seen.

HOMILETICAL INTERPRETATION

In the Gospel for the day we read, "For God sent the Son into the world, not to condemn the world, but that the world might be saved through him" (v. 17). This verse could well serve as the text to sum up the basic themes that run through the three readings for the day. The text assumes that there is reason why God might justly have condemned the world and each of the passages brings out the fact that "men loved darkness rather than light" (v. 19). But even more the readings emphasize that God was not content to let the world drift from him and destroy itself in its darkness. God has continually acted that the world might be saved.

As pointed out in the exegesis, the exodus was the primary divine act in the OT. God acted as the covenant God of the people when he delivered them from out of the degrading slavery into which they had fallen in Egypt. One might hope that the people would be eternally thankful for God's act in delivering them. But alas, that would not have been in keeping with human nature. We forget so quickly the gracious acts of God and his goodness towards us. How quickly, when troubles strike, we complain, "Why did this happen to me?" All of us have our own ideas about how God should govern his universe. And so it is not surprising to find that once delivered from slavery, the people of God began rather quickly to complain about the hardships that they met in freedom. It was not long before some of them wanted to be back with the "fleshpots" of Egypt (Exod. 16:3). In the reading for this day we find that the people were impatient and complained against both God and Moses, their leader.

The writer of Ephesians describes the wondrous gift of salvation that God, in his mercy, has given in Jesus Christ. If the Jews had been delivered from their slavery to the Egyptians, Christians have been delivered from their slavery to sin. One might hope that the Christians would be eternally

The Fourth Sunday in Lent

grateful. When the passage concludes with the words, "For we are his workmanship, created in Christ Jesus for good works, which God prepared beforehand, that we should walk in them," (v. 10) we can only say "Amen!" We who have known the wondrous grace of God in Christ surely ought to give our lives to walking in Christ's spirit and way.

But even as the Jews looked back longingly to the fleshpots of Egypt and complained about God, Christians consistently have failed to walk in the good works for which God has prepared them in Christ. In the NT itself we know that the church was torn with acrimonious debate, backbiting, and unseemly disunity (e.g., see 1 Cor. 1:11-13; Gal. 1:6-7). Gross immorality appeared in the church and was tolerated (1 Cor. 5:1-2). Even among Christians themselves there was a lack of love (e.g., 1 Cor. 6:1-5), and the Lord's Supper became an occasion for a selfish expression of disregard for each other (1 Cor. 11:18-22). Down through history the church has failed miserably to walk in the way prepared for it in Christ. Christians have stained their name with bloody crusades that were fought for no good purpose and included wanton murder, rapine, and theft. They have sided with the exploiters against the exploited. They have supported racial and sexual exploitation. They have persecuted and cast out fellow Christians for difference in doctrine or practice. Truly, as the day's Gospel says, we have loved darkness rather than light.

In all three of our readings, therefore, we are reminded that the behavior of the world has been such that God would have been fully justified if he had simply acted in judgment upon it. But the basic theme of all three readings is that God has never been content to act simply in judgment. God has never desired the destruction of sinful persons, he has always sought their reform and renewal.

In the OT Lesson, the complaints of the people against God result in a plague of poisonous snakes. Surely the ingratitude of the people was such that they deserved what they were getting. But God was not content to let the situation continue. Moses was directed to make a bronze snake that would enable the people to survive the poisonous bites of the living snakes. The marvel of the story is that the only thing required of the people was that they should look at the bronze snake and they would be preserved. Surely, if you or I had been setting the requirements, we would not have let the thankless people off so easily. Most of us would have said, "If you do penance for your ingratitude, if you quit complaining, if you show some thanks, then the bronze serpent will save you." But God did not set up such requirements, the people were delivered simply by looking at the snake.

In the reading from John's Gospel we find a direct comparison drawn between Moses lifting up the bronze snake and the "lifting up" of Christ himself (v. 14). As looking upon the bronze snake saved the Jews from death, so belief in Christ delivers the believer. As the Second Lesson for the day sums it up, "For by grace you have been saved through faith; and this is not your own doing, it is the gift of God..." (v. 8). The three readings bear the same message and yet it is a most difficult one for us to accept. How can God let the guilty Jews off by simply looking at the bronze serpent? Why does he not demand first a change in attitudes? How can God's grace bring salvation through faith? Should God not require that people set their lives straight and reform their behavior before they can be saved?

We begin to see God's point when we meditate upon the fact that "God sent the Son into the world, not to condemn the world, but that the world might be saved." God is not primarily interested in punishing or destroying sinners. His primary concern is that sinners be saved. But salvation does not simply mean a rescue from destruction or punishment, it means a new life of fellowship with God. It means entering into the parent-child relationship that God seeks to have with his children. It means that we become so motivated by our love for God who first loved us that we do his will gladly and freely. But if this is God's goal, could any other method achieve it than the one God has chosen?

Let us look again at the situation of the Jews in the wilderness. The threat of death by snake bite would have a powerful motivation upon the people. In fact, it did move them to see a relationship between their sin and the plague of snakes. God had an opportunity to put great pressure upon the people. He could have offered them a bargain whereby those who repented, cleaned up their lives and generally behaved themselves, would be preserved from death by snakebite. But in that case the change in behavior would have been motivated by fear and self-interest alone. The people would not be truly changed, they would not be motivated by love for God. Despite the fact that their behavior might be changed by their fear, they would still be curved in upon themselves. Fear and the desire to escape punishment can do wonders to change outward behavior but it cannot change the inner motivation of the heart. And therefore it cannot bring about the kind of salvation that God desires.

So God makes no bargain with his people. He offers them the bronze serpent, that anyone who looks at it will live. The bronze serpent becomes a concrete symbol of God's forgiving love and concern for his people. No doubt many will accept God's grace with relief to know that they have

The Fourth Sunday in Lent

nothing further to fear from the snakes and so they will continue to grumble against God. The later history of the people makes it clear that sin did not disappear from their midst because of God's grace. But some did truly repent and believe because of God's gracious act. The way of God's grace bringing salvation through faith is not one that will be universally successful. Paul found that people in his time used God's grace as an excuse to sin so that grace might abound (Rom. 6:1). It might even seem that God is taking a rather dangerous gamble in acting with grace rather than punishment and judgment. But the point is that although grace through faith may not always succeed, no other way can ever succeed.

The success that God seeks is never a matter of outward behavior. In our readings for Ash Wednesday we saw that God calls his people to rend their hearts and not their garments. That is, the outward forms of repentance are meaningless if they are not performed for the right reasons. The change of the "heart," that is the inner self of a person, only comes when people are drawn out of themselves by a love that comes from beyond them. In the wilderness the bronze serpent was a symbol of such a love. But the full meaning of love only comes home to us when we realize that "God so loved the world that he gave his only Son, that whoever believes in him should not perish but have eternal life" (John 3:16).

The Fifth Sunday in Lent

Lutheran	Roman Catholic	Episcopal	Pres./UCC/Chr.	Methodist/COCU
Jer. 31:31-34	Jer. 31:31-34	Jer. 31:31-34	Jer. 31:31-34	Jer. 31:31-34
Heb. 5:7-9	Heb. 5:7-9	Heb. 5:7-9	Heb. 5:7-10	Heb. 5:7-10
John 12:20-33	John 12:20-33	John 12:20-33	John 12:20-33	John 12:20-33

EXEGESIS

First Lesson: Jer. 31:31-34. Jer. 31:31-34, once often judged to be late (and inferior), is now widely held to report faithfully an oracle by Jeremiah even though the words may be those of Baruch, the prophet's secretary and companion.

The phrase "behold, the days are coming" is characteristic of predictions of an indefinite (often eschatological) future. The ejaculation "utterance of Yahweh" repeated in each verse, indicates the prophet's certainty that he is proclaiming God's word and not his own opinion (cf. Jer. 2:2-29; 31:10-20, etc., and cp. 28:5-9). Jeremiah is the herald proclaiming God's "new covenant" with the nation. A covenant was an agreement between two parties which could be entered into by mutual consent (if the parties were equal) or by the imposition by the stronger of his will on the weaker. Often in the OT, God, the stronger, proffers man, the weaker, a covenant in such a way that man is free to accept it or to reject it. Not so here, as will be seen.

The former covenant, based upon the exodus, is described as a marriage contract (v. 32) which had been made null and void by Israel's faithlessness. (Cf. also Jer. 2:2; 3:6-13 where the Lord is pictured as a husband. The AT in v. 32, "so that I had to reject them," translates an emendation based on the Greek and Old Latin. The Hebrew text is intelligible without emendation.)

There is no suggestion in Jer. 31:31-34 that the laws of the old covenant were wrong. The new covenant differs from the old only in that it will be written on the nation's heart, i.e., in the will (cf. the discussion of the heart in the exegesis of Joel 2:12 f. for Ash Wednesday). The new covenant will not have to be taught. No one will have to urge another to obey it.

Jeremiah used the Hebrew root *ydh* (to know) to describe the relationship with God in the new covenant. This root, often used in Hosea (2:20; 4:1, 6; 5:4; 6:6, etc.) and Jeremiah (2:8; 4:22; 9:3, 6; 22:15 f., etc.) also

The Fifth Sunday in Lent 43

described sexual relationships in marriage (as in Gen. 4:1, 17, 25). It conveyed a sense of intimate, intense, mutual involvement. The Israelites' wills will be so changed by the inauguration of the new covenant given by God that they all will know him without instruction, urging, or punishment. Because they will live in intimate fellowship with him, he will forgive the sins that no longer will alienate them from him.

Jer. 31:31-34 is quoted in Heb. 8:8-12 in a description of the new covenant within which Christ officiates as the heavenly high priest. The term "the new covenant" (Jer. 31:31) appears in the sentences pronounced during the Last Supper as reported by Paul (1 Cor. 11:25).

Second Lesson: Heb. 5:7-9. Even though Christ, the heavenly high priest, is the Son of God (1:2—2:9), he also must be human in order to mediate between God and man (2:11-18; 4:15 f.; 5:1-4). Heb. 5:7-9 is the exposition of the humanity of Christ.

V. 7 refers to the prayer of Christ in the Garden of Gethsemane (Mark 14:34-36 = Matt. 26:39 = Luke 22:42). The phrase "with loud cries and tears" is lacking in the Gospels but may either have been taken from an independent tradition or have been a natural expansion of Jesus' words as reported in Mark 14:34. V. 7 ends with an elliptical clause. The Greek reads, "being heard from (*apo*) his reverence (*eulaleia*)." If the preposition *apo* be given a causative force, the various modern translations result. Since it is the human Christ that is being discussed, the implication of the phrase is that all who pray in reverence (or godly fear) will be heard.

The report of the prayer in Gethsemane in Mark implies that Christ sought to escape his crucifixion. This petition was denied (so v. 8 implies), even though it was a Son of God who prayed. Thus the divine-human Christ learned the obedience required of men and women. There is no suggestion that the human Christ was sinful (cf. 4:15). He participated in our humanity by sharing with us temptation and our need to be obedient to the will of God. The divine-human Christ sharing humanity's finitude contrasts with the impassivity of deity in Greek philosophy, but it would not have been alien to participants in the Hellenistic mystery religions with which Christianity was in competition. As a result of his obedience, Christ is made the agency for man's salvation.

Gospel: John 12:20-33. John 12:20-33 is a decisive turning-point in this Gospel. Prior to v. 23, the time for Jesus' passion had not yet come (John 2:4; 7:30; 8:20). Now it has. The earthly ministry carried on among the Jews is to become the ministry of the risen Christ to all peoples. The passage contains three closely related parts: the report of the interest of Greeks in Jesus (vv. 20-22); sayings about the nature of discipleship to the risen Lord (vv. 23-26); and a description of the means by which Jesus' ministry will become available to all people (vv. 27-32).

The "Greeks" coming to worship in Jerusalem during the Passover (v. 20) may have been "God fearers," non-Jews attracted to the ethical monotheism of Judaism who did not accept fully the demands of the law. Their appearance and their desire to see Jesus indicates that interest in his ministry has broken out of the confines of Judaism. Philip and Andrew are reported as being the intermediaries, possibly because of their Greek names (and Philip's home as reported here), or possibly because both disciples may have been related to a church in Asia Minor in which this Gospel may have been written (i.e., Ephesus. A letter by Polycrates, bishop of Ephesus from 189-198 reports Philip's death in a community near Ephesus, and Andrew is linked with the churches in Asia Minor by Eusebius, *Ecclesiastical History* III i.1).

The Greeks are not mentioned again, and the answer to their request is given only indirectly. Vv. 23-26 describe the circumstances in which Gentiles might "see" Jesus. The Son of man must first die in order to be glorified (v. 24). Then those who wish to see Jesus must surrender themselves to him as fully as he had surrendered himself to the will of God that he be crucified (vv. 25, 26a). Such persons will then become servants of Christ and be where he is (v. 26b). Thus it is the risen Christ whom the Gentiles may see.

"Glory" often has the meaning of reputation or status in the OT (cf. Exod. 33:18 f.; Job 19:9; 1 Chron. 16:29. Cp. Exod. 24:16 where a different meaning is required). A person's reputation is a record of his or her acts. Habitual action discloses one's nature. Thus the glory of the Lord to be revealed in the restoration of the exiles (Isa. 40:5) is his nature as a God of redemptive power because this restoration is like earlier divine acts on behalf of Israel. So here also. Christ's nature (his "glory") cannot be disclosed until he is released by the resurrection to do his work fully. His death must precede his glorification, and Jesus can move toward this now that Greeks have become interested in him. In this Gospel, Jesus cannot have been crucified without his consent (John 10:18).

The aphorism in v. 24 may have been intended to refer both to Jesus and to his followers. It has no parallel in the Synoptics (but cf. 1 Cor. 15:36). The saying in v. 25 has parallels in Mark 8:35 = Matt. 10:39; 16:25 = Luke 9:24; 17:33, although the settings and the words used differ. The point being made is the same in all, however. Complete surrender to Jesus and to the way of his cross is opposed to the cultivation of one's own life in this world. The outcome of devotion to Christ is "eternal life." "Life (*psyche*, here equivalent to the Hebrew *nephesh*) in this world" is placed over against "eternal life" (*zoen aionion*), just as "loving" contrasts with "hating," and "losing" with "keeping." V. 26b lacks any parallel in the Synoptics, but note Eph. 2:6 (cf. the exegesis of the Second Lesson for Lent 4).

V. 27 opens with an echo of the scene in Gethsemane reported in the Synoptics. Here, the hint of the struggle of the earthly Jesus against his approaching death becomes the occasion for a statement of Jesus' complete acceptance of his role. He prays for God to act rather than to escape from the crucifixion. One's name epitomized one's essence. For God to glorify his name is for him to act wholly in character, i.e., to do that upon which the redemption of mankind depends. The divine answer is the assurance that God has so acted (in Jesus' ministry) and will again so act (in Jesus' passion, resurrection, and ascension).

Vv. 29 f. record a typical Johannine device. Responding to the reactions of the onlookers becomes the means by which a clarification of meaning is given. Thunder was regarded as the voice of God in Jewish tradition (cf. Exod. 19:19!). If the comment attributed to the people present be read in the light of this tradition, Jesus' reply (v. 30) becomes the means by which his standing before God is doubly affirmed. Jesus did not need a divine attestation to himself, but the people did need to be persuaded of his standing before God.

John 12:20-31 reaches its climax in the two declarations in vv. 31 f. V. 31 is the mirror image of v. 32. The hour has come (v. 23). The iterative emphasis of "now is . . . now is . . ." in English translations of v. 31 is a faithful rendition of the Greek. The judgment (*krisis*: decision or judgment) is in contrapuntal actions by God: the expulsion of the Evil One who rules this age (a divine being over against God; cf. John 8:44; 13:27; 14:30; 2 Cor. 4:4, etc.), and the elevation of Christ (*hypsoun*; cf. the exegesis of John 3:14 in the Gospel for Lent 5). The repudiation of life in this world and the choice of eternal life (vv. 25 f.) is the human response to those divine acts. In v. 33, the evangelist makes it clear that he has been speaking about the crucifixion. Other methods of execution, such as stoning, would not have been described as being lifted up.

HOMILETICAL INTERPRETATION

We are moving through Lent and are coming closer to Palm Sunday, Holy Week, Good Friday, and Easter. It is fitting, therefore, that the readings for this day direct our thoughts to the new covenant that is ushered in by the life, death, and resurrection of Jesus. The word "testament" means "covenant," so the division of the Bible into Old and New Testament is a witness to the importance of the concept of the covenant relationship between God and his people. As the exegesis points out, the concept of a new covenant probably originated with this passage from Jeremiah.

The new covenant is not completely different from the old and certainly it does not contradict it. Jesus said that he had come to fulfill and not destroy the law (Matt. 5:17). In a similar way the new covenant is the fulfillment of the old. The covenant began when God called Abraham to be the father of a people through whom all nations would be blessed (Gen. 12:1-3). It was confirmed and renewed when God delivered his people from slavery in Egypt, gave them his commandments, brought them to the promised land and rescued them from the exile. Jeremiah likens the covenant relationship between God and his people to the covenant relationship of a man and wife (v. 32). But, Jeremiah notes, Israel has been an unfaithful spouse in its marriage relationship to God.

When a marriage has been broken by the unfaithfulness of one of the parties there may be a renewal of the marriage. If the injured party is willing to forgive and the guilty party is willing to accept forgiveness a new relationship may come about. In one sense it is the same marriage as before, but because of the lessons that have been learned, because costly forgiveness has been extended and received, the marriage relationship has been put upon a new level. Jeremiah has such an analogy in mind as he speaks of the new covenant that God will make with his people. God, the injured party, is prepared to forgive so that the covenant relationship can be renewed.

The full nature of the new covenant, of course, cannot be found in Jeremiah. Although Jeremiah heard God's promise that there would be a new covenant, the full implications of it could not be seen until after the life, death, and resurrection of Christ. Nonetheless, Jeremiah has some important clues that we can see fulfilled in Christ.

First, Jeremiah says that God will write the laws upon the hearts of the people. This, of course, is contrasted with the old covenant in which the laws were written on tablets of stone. Under the old covenant God's laws were given by God's gracious love as the way in which the people could respond to God in the covenant relationship. But when the people became unfaithful to God they came to see the law as something over against them, a demand that had to be fulfilled. As we saw in the discussion of the

The Fifth Sunday in Lent

readings for the Third Sunday in Lent, the laws came to be seen as a barrier between God and his people rather than a means of communication.

By the time of Jesus it was all too apparent that the law had become a burden that divided the people from both God and each other. Many of the people seem to have given up hope of ever keeping the law. They were the sinners and outcasts of Jesus' society with whom he mixed so freely. Others, however, were doing a pretty good job of keeping the law in comparison with the "sinners." As a result, they were filled with pride and thanked God that they were not like their sinful neighbors (Luke 18:9-14). To such a situation the promise of the new covenant is a promise that the law will not be seen as an external command to be fulfilled in order to make oneself righteous. Instead, the people will be filled with a desire to do God's will. This happens when Jesus is lifted up on the cross and draws people to himself (John 12:32). The love of God revealed in the death of Christ moves the hearts of people to an answering love. In this relationship there is a true desire to do that which will please God. The law is written on their hearts. Jeremiah foresaw that this desire to keep the law would arise out of a relationship in which "I will be their God, and they shall be my people" (v. 33). We see this relationship established through Christ and his work.

The second clue that Jeremiah gives is that in the new covenant "no longer shall each man teach his neighbor. . ." (v. 34). There would seem to be two implications in this. First, it implies that in the new covenant there shall be no elite group who are experts in the faith and have the duty of passing it on to others. It is not for the clergy, the theologians, or the elect to go out and "save souls." It is God himself who shall make himself known. As Luther put it in his Small Catechism, "I believe that by my own reason or strength I cannot believe in Jesus Christ, my Lord, or come to him. But the Holy Spirit has called me through the Gospel, enlightened me with his gifts, and sanctified and perserved me in true faith, just as he calls, gathers, enlightens and sanctifies the whole Christian church on earth and preserves it in union with Jesus Christ in the one true faith." This comes about because, as we read in the Hebrews' passage, Christ has become our "high priest" (v. 10). The priest is one who mediates between God and the people and so Christ has become the mediator between God and his people.

In the second place, the absence of one person teaching another has implications about the relationship to the will of God. Where the law is seen as a barrier to be overcome to get to God, it results in judgment of others. Because we have kept the law to some degree we thank God that we are not like those who have not done so well in keeping the law. When we take it upon ourselves to teach the law to another there is an implicit implication of judgment. We are the ones who have and keep the law and those we teach are lesser breeds without the law. Luther says that everyone who is apart from Christ ends up passing judgment upon others. Perhaps so, because if we feel that we have to earn our way to God by being righteous, we need some evidence that we are passing the test. Since none of us can claim perfection, the best evidence that we can usually get for our own righteousness is to find someone who is less righteous than ourselves. We look around with a critical eye at our neighbors so that we can assure ourselves that we are not too bad. On the other hand, when we know that we stand before God because of his goodness and not because of our own, we dare to see that we are fellow sinners with our neighbors. We are not in the position to cast the first stone.

This leads us to the third clue that Jeremiah gives us about the new covenant. The law shall be in people's hearts and one shall not have to teach his neighbor because God promises "I will forgive their iniquity, and I will remember their sin no more" (v. 34). This is a wondrous promise. In human relationships we do sometimes forgive those who have injured us. But all too often we do not forget what has been forgiven and we do not let the forgiven party forget it either. As a result, the misdeed hangs like the skeleton in the closet, it remains a barrier between us. Worst of all, we remember the forgiven act so that we can use it as a lever at some future date when we shall work upon the gratitude of the forgiven ones so that we can bend them to our will. God's forgiveness is not of that kind. When we are forgiven the sin is forgotten, it is past and obliterated.

In the new covenant we are shown that forgiving and forgetting is a costly process. The short passage from Hebrews brings to mind in a few words the agony that Jesus experienced in Gethsemane. To be the high priest that mediates between God and his people, Jesus had to learn obedience through what he suffered (v. 8). In the Gospel we see the same thing, as Jesus indicates that his soul is troubled (v. 27). He does not even know how to pray. Shall he ask to be delivered from this hour? No, it is for this hour that he has been sent. And so he anticipates his being raised upon the cross. Salvation may be free, but it is not cheap.

Throughout Lent our assigned readings have reminded us of God's covenant relationship with his people. Because God loved us he sought for us. He entered into the covenant relationship which we have broken time and time again. But God did not give up on us. As Karl Barth says, we may give up on God and become atheist but God never gives up on us and becomes a humanist. And so it is that to those who have failed to keep the old covenant there comes the promise of a new covenant. We stand today in the new covenant, remembering that it was instituted by the sacrifices of God in Christ. The church exists today, the people of God, as a fulfillment of Christ's promise: "and I, when I am lifted up from earth, will draw all men to myself" (v. 32).